Fort Moultrie
Constant Defender

Jim Stokeley

Produced by the
Division of Publications
National Park Service

U.S. Department of the Interior
Washington, D.C. 1985

About This Book
From 1776 until the end of World War II, the guns of
Fort Moultrie helped protect the sea approaches to
the important commercial city of Charleston, South
Carolina. Twice the fort was caught up in the
whirlwind of war, and the battles it fought are now a
worthy part of the Nation's military annals. From
1794 on, it was a significant part of a cohesive
national system of seacoast defenses, and the succes-
sive generations of fortifications on this site clearly
show the delicate interplay between the demands of
geography, technological advances in weaponry, and
the peculiarly American tendency to seek security
through armaments requiring a minimum of man-
power. Jim Stokely's vivid account sketches this
uneven march of men and events at Fort Moultrie
and illuminates an important aspect of America's
military tradition. For the story of Moultrie's com-
panion defender of Charleston Harbor, Fort Sumter,
see National Park Handbook No. 127.

National Park Handbooks, compact introductions to
the great natural and historic places administered by
the National Park Service, are published to support
the National Park Service's management programs
at the parks and to promote understanding and
enjoyment of the parks. This is Handbook No. 136.

Library of Congress Cataloging in Publication Data
Stokely, Jim
Constant Defender.
Bibliography: p.
1. Moultrie, Fort, S.C.—History. I. Title.
F279.C48M687   975.7'91   77-608144

ISBN 0-912627-27-1

Part 1

Guardian at the Straits

The Story of Fort Moultrie

In the spring of 1663, eight court favorites persuaded England's King Charles II to grant them "all America from sea to sea between the 36 and 31 parallels of latitude under the name of Carolina." This gift to the Lords Proprietors of Carolina turned out to be somewhat larger and more important than originally expected.

The proprietors dreamed of a peaceful colony for themselves, a landed aristocracy, a prosperous society of manors and manners. In time, English sugar planters from the West Indies—especially from the over-crowded Caribbean island of Barbados—arrived and established their estates. Others less wealthy and more mobile came also: dissenters from New England, French Huguenots, hard-working Germans, and a smattering of Welsh, Spanish, and Scotch-Irish. The chief settlement here came to be called Charles Town—renamed Charleston in 1783—and was located at the confluence of the Ashley and Cooper Rivers. The colony grew, elected its own assembly, and inevitably crossed purposes with the rule of the Lords Proprietors. In 1719, a rebellion in the city overthrew the proprietary governor, and 10 years later the proprietors surrendered their charter to the Crown.

Under the more relaxed rule of the Crown, the economy of the Carolina Low Country developed at a rapid rate. Settlers tamed the swamplands and grew vast quantities of rice, and great plantations began to dot the countryside. When market prices fell during the 1740s, planters turned to indigo, famous for its blue dye, and discovered that this summer plant, which grew well in the loamy soil, complemented their rice culture. For the next 30 years, prices on these staples rose steadily, and the fortunes of South Carolina's planters soared. As the only major city south of Philadelphia, Charleston assumed an increasing commercial importance. And it was propitiously situated at the mouth of a major

Capt. Barnard Elliott's elegant dress belied his prowess as a fighter. In September 1775 he led a company of the 2nd South Carolina Regiment in the seizure of Fort Johnson on James Island, capturing vast stores of Royal cannon and supplies. Promoted to lieutenant colonel, he commanded the North Battery during the June 28, 1776, attack on Charleston.

river, available both to overseas shipping routes and to a vigorous overland trade with the Up Country. In this position Charleston could turn another healthy profit from inland meat, grain, and animal skins shipped abroad or to other colonies.

By the early 1770s, with a full century of settlement behind it, this thriving urban center had come into its own. Its 12,000 residents—the half of them who were white—looked optimistically to the future. Henry Laurens, for instance, was a saddler's son who, through reasonably hard work as a merchant, amassed more than 20,000 acres. And there was Thomas Nightingale, becoming richer each day operating a race track, sponsoring auctions and cock fights, leasing wagons, and "entertaining Indians" at public expense to encourage the back country trade. This was a young society, enthusiastic and on the move, a mixture of nationalities and cultural styles. "Their whole Lives are one continued Race," wrote a local newspaper, with only a little exaggeration. "Every Tradesman is a Merchant, every Merchant is a Gentleman; and every Gentleman one of the Noblesse."

The blurred distinction between classes stood Charleston in good stead. Although each class naturally looked out for its own interests, growing dissatisfaction with British manipulation gradually transformed the many into one. Needing funds to maintain its far-flung army and navy after the French and Indian War, Britain had heightened its mercantilistic policies of taxation on the colonies and restriction of American manufacturing. As the years went by and the Crown's directives accumulated— the Sugar Act, the Stamp Act, the Quartering Act, the Townsend Duties, and the Tea Act—many of Charleston's planter-aristocrats chafed under such distant domination. Charleston merchants disliked regulations limiting their businesses and taxing their profits. And the city's large body of artisans, many of whom operated their own enterprises, took a dim view of these controls. Clothiers and carpenters, chandlers and coachmakers, bricklayers and gunsmiths, and a host of other artisans hated a system that jammed British products down their throats.

The antagonisms took on a momentum of their own. As early as 1768, Charlestonians had gathered under the Liberty Oak "in Mr. Mazyck's pasture" and "spent a few hours in a new round of toasts, among which, scarce a celebrated Patriot of Britain or America was omitted." In September 1774, five South Carolina representatives journeyed north to Philadelphia and took part in the first Continental Congress. A month later Charleston threw a Boston-like Tea Party where, "with ominous dignity," patriots suggested that local importers of British East Indian tea might want to dump that tea into the waters of Charleston Harbor—and they did.

The lines were drawn. A Provincial Congress controlled by patriots met in January 1775 and assumed legislative authority in the Low Country. On May 8, Charleston received word of the confrontation in April at Lexington and Concord. Patriots and Loyalists, rich and poor, planter and journeyman, suddenly realized that for better or worse, the time for fighting was upon them.

Col. William Thomson, one-time Indian trader and indigo planter, rendered great service at Fort Moultrie in June 1776 when, with his Rangers, a regiment of mounted infantry, he blocked the British attempt to land on Sullivans Island.

Revolution and Independence

The Provincial Congress met again on June 1. It encouraged the officers of a dozen existing militia regiments to hold their men in readiness, and it authorized payment for three regiments of regular soldiers. Col. Christopher Gadsden, a strong and outspoken patriot, was elected to lead the 1st South Carolina Regiment of Infantry. Col. William Moultrie, a stout, ruddy Charlestonian with a bulldog jaw, headed the 2d Regiment. Col. William Thomson, a popular Scotch-Irishman born in Pennsylvania and raised on a frontier farm in South Carolina, commanded the mounted infantry Regiment of Rangers. Each infantryman was paid one shilling a day, the rangers receiving more because they were responsible for the care of their horses. These regiments attracted the prominent names of the Low Country: Captains Pinckney, Lynch, Richardson; 1st Lieutenants Drayton, Dickenson, Middleton, Mason, Motte, Huger, and one Francis Marion.

Immediately after the regiments were authorized, a group of "confidential gentlemen" sailed to the Caribbean in schooners and returned with 10,000 pounds of powder, which seemed to Moultrie "a very seasonable supply." In August, regimental offi-

London of the Low Country

"The people of Charleston," wrote a visitor to that colonial metropolis, "live rapidly, not willingly letting go untasted any of the pleasures of life." For Charleston's wealthy, the daily routine could be very kind indeed. A trio of theaters, expensive and well-attended, offered such plays as John Dryden's *All For Love* and Shakespeare's *King Lear.* Music societies, such as the exclusive St. Cecilia, provided formal concerts and contributed to a vital atmosphere which nurtured some of America's best actors and musicians. Clubs and race tracks thrived for the men and Josiah Quincy of Boston noted that the ladies especially liked "Music and Dancing, which it must be confessed, make them very agreeable Companions, but will render them expensive Wives." Sons received their education at Oxford, Cambridge, and other European universities.

The Charleston Museum was founded in 1773 and devoted itself to preserving the high style of the city's life. Charleston's streets were graced by splendid brick homes in the Georgian style, with elaborate piazzas, iron balconies, and furnishings on the order of "azure blue window curtains, rich blue paper with gilt, mashee borders, most elegant pictures, excessive grand and costly looking glasses." Public buildings and churches reflected the Charleston aesthetic.

Such stately elegance was partly offset by a robust urban turmoil. One cabinetmaker, the victim of complaints by a competitor, distributed an advertisement

concerning the fellow's observations and noted that "his Customers for the Future will pay no Regard to the Words of such a low groveling malicious Fellow, pregnant with impudence, Ignorance, and Falsehoods, and who is too insignificant a Creature to have his name mentioned in a public Paper."

The more sophisticated side of Charleston life rested upon this seemingly chaotic but nevertheless successul economic base. Charleston shipwrights, for example, made expensive vessels of high quality. Their sloops, schooners and brigantines, constructed solidly of oak, sold for much more than those of Massachusetts and Philadelphia, where labor was cheaper. But many merchants from cities like Glasgow, Edinburgh, and London still preferred to own a Carolina-built ship. In all probability, they would not have minded moving themselves across the waters and making a new life in this congenial city.

Charleston's prosperity is reflected in the view below, painted by artist Thomas Leitch in 1771, on the eve of the American Revolution. Its portrayal of an active and thriving seaport also helps to reinforce the city's claim to be the "London of the Low Country."

cers set out on successful recruiting trips to North Carolina, Virginia, and the back country. One of these recruiters was Capt. Barnard Elliott. An elegant product of English education who wore silk stockings, he drew the ridicule of many a rawboned backcountryman. When the settlers at one crossroads stood unswayed by the usual blandishments of money, drink, and music, Elliott learned that their stocky leader "never could think of serving under a man that he could lick." Captain Elliott challenged the fellow to a fight and lost no time in showing him another result of British education: the art of boxing. The countryman and his neighbors enlisted.

These recruits funneled into Charleston and received essential support from the city. Townspeople had already broken into the local armory, and many of Charleston's artisans were hired to furnish additional supplies: clothing, tools, and saddles. Throughout the fall of 1775, while militiamen skirmished with Loyalist bands in the upcountry, Charlestonians worked to drive two British sloops from the harbor. Cannon appeared on the waterfront where old warehouses had been. Patriots seized Fort Johnson, located southeast of the city on James Island. A heavy battery went up across the water at Haddrell Point, and when a crew began to place guns at the mouth of the harbor on Sullivans Island, the British ships— with the royal governor on board—sailed away.

Despite such initial rebuffs throughout the colonies, the British devised a plan that they hoped would cripple resistance to the Crown. The bulk of the British forces in America, commanded by Sir William Howe, would march against the middle colonies. A smaller Southern force would consist of units dispatched from Howe's army, additional troops from England that would sail directly to the Carolinas, and a large number of Southern Loyalists who would help the cause on their own ground. Howe selected Maj. Gen. Henry Clinton to lead the Southern Expedition. Sir Peter Parker was named to command the expedition's naval force gathering at Cork, Ireland. In late January Clinton sailed from Boston with 1,500 men, bound for Cape Fear on the coast of North Carolina.

By February 1776, John Rutledge had returned to Charleston from a long session with the Continental Congress. He brought back warnings of a British

Maj. Gen. Henry Clinton, second in command of the British Army in America, was sent south to restore the King's authority in Virginia, North Carolina, South Carolina, and Georgia. When a series of British defeats denied him the Loyalist support he needed to carry out his mission, he focused his attention on Charleston. Ironically, he ended up as a spectator during the naval attack on Fort Moultrie (then called Fort Sullivan) when his troops were unable to cross the Breach at the eastern edge of Sullivans Island.

move in the South. Well-educated, eloquent and a forceful persuader, Rutledge was soon elected president of a newly formed General Assembly that became and remained the backbone of South Carolina's revolutionary government. That government was soon to be tested, for when Clinton reached the Cape Fear River in March, he learned that a sizable body of North Carolina Loyalists had been soundly defeated at Moores Creek Bridge on February 27. Clinton reviewed the British plan and waited for Parker, who arrived in early May. Their eyes now turned toward Charleston.

Under Rutledge's leadership, the city steadily strengthened its defenses. Because of the extended absence of Gadsden, a member of the Continental Congress, Rutledge placed the direction of Charleston's military preparations in the hands of 46-year-old Col. William Moultrie, former militiaman and Indian fighter. Three days after the battle at Moores Creek, Moultrie was ordered to Sullivans Island to supervise the building of a "large fort" there. From the beginning, the fortification was intended for seacoast defense. Its purpose was to make an invasion as costly as possible, or, better still, to prevent an invader from landing at all. Since such a fixed defensive position could not reasonably be expected to annihilate the enemy, the fort would have to be backed up by inland troops and a well-armed city.

Sullivans Island was thought to be the key to this geographically shielded harbor. A large vessel sailing into Charleston first had to cross Charleston Bar, a series of submerged sand banks lying about 8 miles southeast of the city. A half-dozen channels penetrated the bar, but only the southern pair could be navigated by deep-draft ships. A broad anchorage called Five Fathom Hole lay between the bar and Morris Island. From Five Fathom Hole shipping headed northward before turning west. At this point the channel narrowed considerably. To the south, a well-known shoal, called the Middle Ground, projected outward from James Island. Although part of this sand bank would later provide the site for Fort Sumter, its main significance over the years lay in its existence as an obstacle that influenced defensive strategy within the harbor. Just a thousand yards north of the shoal loomed the crucial southern end of Sullivans Island.

The island's very name harked back to the rigors of defense. In 1674 one Captain O'Sullivan had been appointed to maintain a signal cannon here and to fire it as any vessel approached. The site of Moultrie's fort, close by the shoreline to the south, was indeed a strategic one, overlooking the channel into Charleston. A ship had to approach it bow first until within close range, then turn to port and expose her stern as she passed the fort. The ship would have very little time to fire broadside and would herself be raked fore and aft. When Moultrie and his 2d South Carolina Regiment arrived on site in early March 1776, they found a "great number of mechanics and negroe laborers" already at work on the fort. South Carolina's revolutionary government authorized two rifle regiments for reinforcements, to be commanded by Isaac Huger and Thomas Sumter.

Adm. Peter Parker commanded the British naval forces in the attack on Charleston. He was later knighted for his bravery there, and he eventually became Admiral of the Fleet, the senior British naval officer.

Moultrie and his men joined a detachment on the island under Capt. Peter Horry. Horry had made sure that a pair of British warships, *Tamar* and *Cherokee*, did not send landing parties ashore. During the next weeks, work gangs cut thousands of spongy palmetto logs and rafted them over from the other sea islands and the mainland. Encouraged and excited, Captain Horry kept a close eye on the fort's progress and likened its design to "an immense pen 500 feet long, and 16 feet wide, filled with sand to stop the shot." The workers constructed gun platforms out of 2-inch planks and nailed them together with spikes. Moultrie himself concluded that "every one was busy, and everything went on with great spirit."

By mid-May, Charlestonians received word of the formidable British fleet at Cape Fear. But they also learned that 2,000 Virginia and North Carolina soldiers, led by Gen. Charles Lee, were marching to the Low Country's assistance. Lt. Felix Walker, from the Watauga country in what later became East Tennessee, recounted how he raised one North Carolina company: *I went to Mecklenburg County, and meeting with some recruiting officers by recommendation of General Thomas Polk, I was appointed Lieutenant in Capt. Richardson's Company in the Rifle Regiment, commanded by Isaac Huger, then a Colonel, and was there furnished with money for the recruiting service. I returned to Watauga and on my way throughout that country I recruited my full*

proportion of men, and marched them to Charles-
town in May. . . .

Young Walker, a budding "over-mountain" man
who had once served an apprenticeship in Charleston, lured his friends and other youthful frontiers-
men with enticing stories of the city and the ocean.
Even though many western North Carolinians stayed
home to buttress their region against the Cherokees,
a sizeable number contributed to Charleston's defense. Some joined Thomson's Rangers, but most
were stationed with Huger in the second line of
defense, between Sullivans Island and the city.

Late in May, the frigate *Sphinx* and the schooner
Pensacola Packet sailed from Cape Fear to recon-
noiter Charleston Harbor. When five of Moultrie's
men went out to the frigate in one of his barges, it
was "hoisted with sails standing athwart the Bowsprit
of the Man of War and [hung] there for a whole
day." This inglorious "hanging" was meant by the
British to impress the townspeople as a "way of
Bravado or perhaps as an innuendo of what they
would do with the Owner, if they could lay their
hands on him." After sending a small party to burn
the ship *St. James*, a British vessel taken prize by the
South Carolina brigantine *Comet*, *Sphinx* and her
tender confidently returned north. Patriots grimly
realized that the main fleet would soon arrive.

Onboard *Bristol*, Clinton and Parker debated the
fleet's future operations. Clinton—confident, aloof
but aggressive, a British aristocrat raised in New
York, the beneficiary of a steady succession of
promotions—studied an attack on Charleston but
leaned toward rejoining Howe's army. Clinton, however, soon received a letter from Howe outlining
plans for a summer campaign against New York City
and the Hudson River Valley. Howe did not call
upon Clinton for "any immediate assistance," but,
pointing out Charleston "as an object of importance
to his Majesty's Service," gave the impression that he
wished him to take some action in the South. New
information concerning "the works erected by the
Rebels of Sullivans Island" indicated that the fort
was "in an imperfect and unfinished state." Upon
learning this, Parker—a more expressive man than
Clinton but just as vain—proposed to "attempt the
reduction of that Fortress by a coup de main." When
Sphinx and *Pensacola Packet* returned from their

reconnaissance, the British made their move. The fleet weighed anchor on May 30, crossed Cape Fear Bar, and stood to the south.

Patriot couriers brought word to Charleston on May 31 that British vessels were seen near Dewees Island, 20 miles away. On June 1, the fleet appeared and "displayed about fifty sail before the town, on the out side of the bar." The ships had been long expected, but their actual presence was, nevertheless, frightening. Moultrie described their effect on Charlestonians: *The sight of these vessels alarmed us very much, all was hurry and confusion, the president with his council busy in sending expresses to every part of the country, to hasten down the militia; men running about the town looking for horses, carriages, and boats to send their families into the country; and as they were going out through the town gates to go into the country, they met the militia from the country marching into town; traverses were made in the principal streets; fleches thrown up at every place where troops could land; military works going on every where, the lead taking [sic] from the windows of the churches and dwelling houses, to cast into musket balls, and every preparation to receive an attack, which was expected in a few days.*

Richard Hutson, militiaman, reached Charleston and remained unimpressed with the regular troops he saw: "I expect that when it comes to the push we shall be obliged to do all ourselves." But Moultrie, watching the British scout out possible landings on nearby Long Island (now called Isle of Palms), wrote to President Rutledge on June 3: "Our fort is now enclosed. It is the opinion of everyone, that we should have more men at this post; but, as I know they cannot be spared from the capital, I must make the best defence I can with what I have got; and doubt not, but that I shall give 4 or 500 men a great deal of trouble before they can dislodge me from this post."

Within days, Gen. Charles Lee arrived at Charleston and Rutledge put him in command of all South Carolina troops. A lean, handsome scholar, Lee carried with him a reputation for eccentricity and brilliance. From his native England, he had journeyed to America during the French and Indian Wars and had immensely liked the new country, with its "spirit of liberty." He married the daughter of a Seneca chief and garnered an Indian name meaning "boiling water." Lee traveled extensively in the colonies, met with their leading figures, and published many pamphlets and essays strongly advocating an American break with Britain. Upon the outbreak of the Revolutionary War, he was considered with Washington for the position of commander-in-chief. Washington considered Lee "the first officer in military knowledge we have in the whole army." General "Boiling Water" was finally persuaded to take the Southern command, but no one knew in what direction he would take it.

The appearance of Lee in Charleston boosted morale immensely. "It was thought by many," said Moultrie, "that his coming among us was equal to a reinforcement of 1000 men." Lee boasted that he would send Clinton a challenge if nothing happened soon. After viewing Charleston's defenses, however, Lee's private worries mounted. He inspected one battery planned by Chief Justice John Drayton and remarked that "he may be a very good Chief Justice but he is a damn bad Engineer." Lee found the soldiers of the 2d South Carolina encamped behind the unfinished fort "in huts and booths covered with palmetto leaves." Thomson's regiment, responsible for maintaining an "Advance Guard" at the northern end of Sullivans Island, was a bit more securely placed among the dunes and the myrtle. Thomson and his 300 Rangers commanded The Breach, a narrow inlet between their position and Long Island. They were to prevent, or if need be harass, any British beachhead on Sullivans Island.

On June 8, after most of the British fleet had crossed the bar and anchored in Five Fathom Hole, Clinton delivered a proclamation to the patriots. He wished to "entreat and exhort them, as they tender their own happiness and that of their posterity, to return to their duty to our common sovereign." Rutledge rejected this plea. A day later, Clinton and 500 soldiers landed on Long Island, and on June 10 Parker's 50-gun flagship, *Bristol*, and the last of his deep-draft transports crossed Charleston Bar. Moultrie immediately moved his men inside the fort, but remained confident. When a visitor to the fort pointed to the British fleet, Moultrie replied, "We should beat them."

"Sir," the visitor said, "when those ships . . . come to lay along side of your fort, they will knock it down in half an hour!"

Moultrie answered coldly, "We will lay behind the ruins and prevent their men from landing."

Lee did not share this confidence. He referred to the fort as a "slaughter pen" of sand and logs, yet Rutledge refused to let him abandon it. Lee ordered Moultrie to build a breastwork of sand inside the works, in case the British stormed the fort. He also began a pet project: a floating bridge of hogsheads and planks stretching across the marshy cove from Sullivans Island to the mainland, which furnished a possible line of retreat. The bridge was never satisfactorily completed, and when 200 of Lt. Col. Thomas Clark's men tested it, the bridge began to sink and the soldiers were forced to scramble for dry land. Finally, Lee placed a 1,500-man force on the mainland at Haddrell Point, near the Cove. Most of his faith in a successful defense rested with the second line, but Moultrie still clung to the fort. One day while inspecting it, Lee brusquely took Moultrie aside and asked him directly: "Do you think you can maintain this post?" "Yes, I think I can," came the reply.

Parker's fleet included transports, victuallers, service vessels, and nine men-of-war—*Bristol, Experiment, Actaeon, Active, Solebay, Syren, Sphinx, Friendship,* and the bomb vessel *Thunder*—mounting nearly 300 heavy guns. By late June, Moultrie commanded 31 cannon and a garrison of less than 400 men, including 20 men from the 4th South Carolina Artillery Regiment. The square-shaped fort, completed only on the seaward front, presented no invincible image. Palmetto walls, 16 feet wide and filled with sand, rose 10 feet above wooden platforms for the soldiers and their guns. A hastily erected palisade of thick planks helped guard the powder magazine and the unfinished northern curtains. A motley assortment of hard-to-get cannon, ranging from 9- and 12-pounders to English 18-pounders and French 26-pounders, dotted the rear breastworks, the southeast and southwest walls, and the corner bastions.

Throughout the Charleston area, troops seemed uneasy as they expected battle. Bothered by mosquitoes and plagued with sickness from "bad drinking

Maj. Gen. Charles Lee, commander of the Charleston defenses during the June 1776 attack, wanted to abandon the fort on Sullivans Island, believing it to be indefensible and a potential "slaughter pen." When John Rutledge, President of the South Carolina General Assembly, insisted it be held, Lee reluctantly agreed.

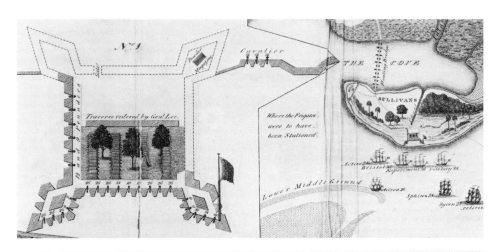

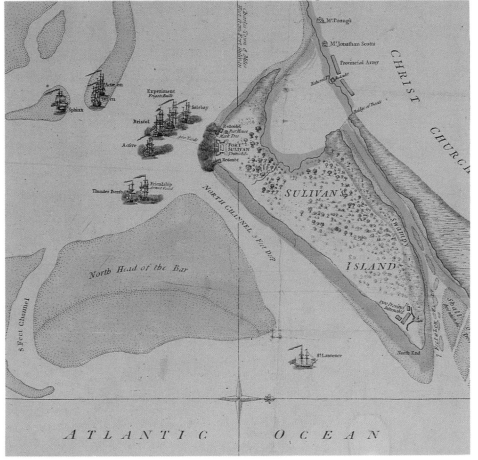

water, constant exposure to the broiling sun during the day and sleeping on the damp ground at night," soldiers chafed and fretted. Some sent up a great "clamore for their pay," while others had to be disciplined with frequent courts-martial. Even officers were strictly held in line. Everyone, including militia and civilians in Charleston, waited impatiently. Moultrie checked with Thomson's Advance Guard, now strengthened with two light cannon and 100 more men, and made sure that the Guard would fall back to the fort should the British successfully cross The Breach.

Meantime, Clinton had increased his force on Long Island. On June 20, he sent Maj. Gen. Charles Cornwallis' brigade—the Earl's first large command of the war—southward to pitch camp within sight of The Breach. But Clinton had also received disappointing news: the depth of The Breach at ebb tide, which he had originally thought to be half-a-yard, was in reality seven feet. Clinton therefore sent notice to Parker that he was considering using boats to land troops inside the harbor, near Haddrell Point or even on the southern end of Sullivans Island. Instead of committing Clinton to a specific plan, Parker left the decision up to him. Thus by the last week in June, the British had leisurely settled on a vague, uncoordinated strategy. Parker's ships would penetrate the harbor, level the fort, and possibly support Clinton in an amphibious assault. Clinton would help out some way, probably by destroying Thomson's Advance Guard and storming the work from the rear.

The British and the patriots were as ready as they could reasonably hope to be. June 24 dawned overcast, and the weather became squally. The 50-gun ship *Experiment* crossed Charleston Bar and joined Parker's fleet on the morning of June 27. Charles Lee kept a steady stream of advice flowing to Moultrie. That night, word circulated through the British fleet that "no quarter would be given the Americans, and that £5,000 had been offered for General Lee." Events pointed toward the 28th as the fateful day.

At 9 a.m., June 28, Parker fired a signal gun. An hour later his warships advanced. The move caught Moultrie conferring with Thomson's Advance Guard, but when lookouts raised the cry that the men-of-war were coming, Moultrie galloped back to the fort.

Lee was at that moment attempting to cross from the mainland to the island, but rough water forced his small boat back. Lee had spent the first half of the morning in Charleston where he had notified Rutledge that he would replace Moultrie with Col. Francis Nash unless Moultrie carried out his orders. Now, however, there remained no time for such dickering. From his vantage point across The Cove, Lee watched the British ships maneuver into firing position.

Thunder and *Friendship* anchored 1½ miles from the fort. Four ships—*Active, Bristol, Experiment,* and *Solebay*—took positions about 400 yards out in a line west to east opposite most of the fort's cannon. The British moved slowly and confidently, fueling the fears of Charlestonians that Parker's looming men-of-war could "knock the town about our ears, notwithstanding our batteries." At 11:30, gunners aboard *Thunder* began to loft 13-inch mortar bombs toward the fort. Moultrie's men began firing on *Active,* the first ship within range, and hit her four or five times. Then came the British broadsides, loud and powerful. Lee called them "the most furious and incessant fires I ever saw or heard." Parker's frigates—*Sphinx, Syren,* and *Actaeon*—now sought to take advantage of this cover fire and sailed past the fort toward The Cove, planning to take up a position from whence they could both attack the fort from its weak side and isolate the island from the mainland. It was a momentous move, yet it failed. The ships' pilots, unfamiliar with the harbor, ran their ships aground on Charleston's infamous sand banks.

Inside the fort, gun crews labored furiously to return the British fire. Moultrie termed the situation "one continual blaze and roar," with "clouds of smoke curling over ... for hours together." The garrison had enough powder on hand for only 28 rounds per gun. Lieutenant Byrd was soon sent to inform Lee of this shortage. The patriots quickly abandoned three poorly protected 12-pounders west of the fort, but the main walls of sand and palmetto stood up well and smothered most of the British bombs before they could explode. Many of the American casualties came from direct hits through the embrasures. The first man killed, Cpl. Samuel Yarbury, was rolled off the platform amid epithets of revenge. About 3 p.m., Moultrie received a dismaying report that Clinton had landed successfully on Sullivans Island.

The information proved false. On the contrary, Thomson's troops had prevented Clinton from doing anything. Although Clinton had long since commenced bombardment of Thomson's position, he knew that the grounding of the three frigates limited his options. When Clinton finally began to move toward The Breach with armed schooners and infantry, the Americans halted their advance. Thomson's artillery raked the British decks, and most of Clinton's foot soldiers never made it to The Breach. A young North Carolinian named Morgan Brown described this engagement: "Our rifles were in prime order, well proved and well charged; every man took deliberate aim at his object. . . . The fire taught the enemy to lie closer behind their bank of oyster shells, and only show themselves when they rose up to fire." Clinton judiciously held his position until nightfall, then cancelled any further attacks. A British crewman onboard a schooner later wrote of Thomson's success: "It was impossible for any set of men to sustain so destructive a fire as the Americans poured in . . . on this occasion."

The battle at the fort was more closely drawn. By mid-afternoon the British had refloated *Sphinx* and *Syren*, although *Actaeon* remained aground. These two ships joined the general bombardment of the fort, which at one point "gave the merlons such a tremor" that Moultrie grew "apprehensive that a few more such would tumble them down." In the midst of the battle, when a British projectile broke the fort's flagstaff, Sgt. William Jasper "lept over the ramparts" and, in the words of Captain Horry, *deliberately walked the whole length of the fort, until he came to the colors on the extremity of the left, when he cut off the same from the mast, and called to me for a sponge staff, and with a thick cord tied on the colors and stuck the staff on the rampart in the sand. The sergeant fortunately received no hurt, though exposed for a considerable time, to the enemy's fire.*

Moultrie had ordered his gun captains to concentrate their fire on *Bristol* and *Experiment*. Men all along the platform cried, "mind the Commodore, mind the two fifty gun ships." As American shot

These watercolors by Lt. Henry Gray of the 2nd South Carolina Regiment depict the action on Sullivans Island, June 28 & 29, 1776. The upper painting shows the ships of Admiral Parker's fleet exchanging fire with the American fort on June 28. In the lower view the grounded British frigate *Acteon* can be seen burning on the day after the attack, while the Americans are returning to shore after boarding the vessel to remove all undamaged sails and stores. Amateur artist Gray completed the paintings while recovering from wounds recieved in the fight, and together they provided a vivid eyewitness view of the battle.

Gray continued to serve in the American army and was promoted to captain in 1778. He was wounded again in 1779, during the siege of Savannah, Ga. His military career ended on May 12, 1780, when he and nearly 5,500 others were captured as Charleston fell to besieging British forces.

ploughed into these men-of-war, Moultrie grew more positive that Parker "was not at all obliged to us for our particular attention to him." Indeed, one round on the *Bristol's* quarterdeck rendered Sir Peter's "Britches ... quite torn off, his backside laid bare, his thigh and knee wounded." In the afternoon's oppressive heat many of the fort's garrison shed their coats. When an exploding bomb slung one of the cast-off coats into a nearby tree, a rumor spread among the British fleet that it was an American deserter, hanged as an example to his fellow soldiers.

Lee visited the fort at 4 p.m. to "encourage the garrison by his presence." About this time another 700 pounds of powder reached the defenders. The powder was more necessary than Lee's presence, as the general soon recognized. Walking about the platforms with "coolness and self possession," Lee found the men "determined and cool to the last Degree, their behaviour would in fact have done honors to the oldest troops." Lee redirected several of the guns, then said to Moultrie: "Colonel, I see you are doing very well here, and you have no occasion for me, so I will go up to town again."

With the extra powder, the patriots fired until sunset and even afterwards sent their shot into the British ships with a deliberate regularity. By 9 p.m. Parker had had enough and withdrew to lick his wounds. The reports came in. Onboard *Bristol,* 40 were dead and 71 wounded. The ship itself was hit 70 times, with "much damage in her Hull, Yards, and Rigging"; *Experiment* also suffered: 23 dead, 56 wounded. There were 15 casualties onboard *Active* and *Solebay.* Against such heavy losses the fort sustained 25 wounded and a dozen killed. The battle of Sullivans Island had required just a single day to play itself out. On the morning of June 29 the British set the grounded *Actaeon* afire and abandoned it. The Americans added insult to defeat by sailing out to the burning ship and briefly firing several of its guns at the departing *Bristol.* After the eager defenders returned to shore, *Actaeon* exploded, sending up an inferno which seemed to Moultrie "a grand pillar of smoke, which soon expanded itself at the top, and to appearance, formed the figure of a palmetto tree."

The British had used 32,000 pounds of powder, the Americans less than 5,000. Moultrie's men later searched Sullivans Island and "gathered up more shot, from 24-pounders down to the smallest size, than they had fired." The fort still stood, as squat and unimposing as ever, but British shot had destroyed almost all of the island's huts and trees. Parker and Clinton evacuated the area in late July and began to blame each other for their defeat. Lee blamed no one but himself for doubting: "The behaviour of the Garrison, both men and officers, with Colonel Moultrie at their head, I confess, astonished me." President Rutledge gave his sword to Sergeant Jasper; Moultrie was later promoted to general, and the fort was named in his honor.

The engagement at Sullivans Island assumed unquestioned importance. Within days of the battle, Charlestonians learned of the signing of the Declaration of Independence. The June 28 victory stood as a kind of physical Declaration, an early sign of the American capacity to oppose the British at arms. As historian Edwin C. Bearss has observed, the colonies had much to cheer: *So far in 1776 General Washington had accomplished little beyond hurrying Howe's evacuation of Boston. The American army sent to overrun and occupy Canada had collapsed. Now came word of a victory from the south. Not only had the British been repulsed before Sullivans Island, but they had given up their initial attempt to carry the war to the southern colonies.* The upsetting of British plans in the South helped win uncommitted Americans to the struggle for independence. It also enabled the Southern colonies to support vital campaigns in the north. Most directly and significantly, the American triumph at Sullivans Island helped keep an important Southern port free from British occupation for more than three years.

When the British returned to Charleston in February 1780, they did so with determination. Fort Moultrie had been strengthened and its walls raised to 20 feet, but the English squadron knew enough not to repeat the mistakes of 1776. British troops landed south of Charleston Harbor and marched overland to capture Fort Johnson. Vice Adm. Marriot Arbuthnot's fleet skirted Sullivans Island on April 8 and anchored in Rebellion Road under the protection of Fort Johnson's guns. Three weeks later British troops were landed at Haddrell Point, and on May 6 a combined British force of sailors and marines offered terms to a besieged Fort Moultrie. The next day, Moultrie's 160-member garrison surrendered. Maj. Patrick Ferguson, one of the British commanders, marched into the bastion and described it as "the strongest Fort ever built by Hands." By mid-May Charleston itself had surrendered to an enemy 14,000 strong.

After nearly four years, the British had finally taken Fort Moultrie. But the tide of the Revolutionary War had shifted in favor of America. This second offensive against the South was Britain's last great effort to subdue the colonies. When the British evacuated Charleston in December 1783 the patriots triumphantly reoccupied Moultrie and stayed until the next summer. The Treaty of Paris, announced April 19, 1784, formally put an end to war and officially recognized the United States of America. Moultrie's garrison soon withdrew and left the fort to "the assaults of man and nature." Severe storms, coupled with human needs for building materials, gradually reduced Fort Moultrie to a wreck. Yet, in time, the fort would rise again.

War and Rumors of War

During the 1790s and the first half of the following century, Fort Moultrie became more than the site of a famous Revolutionary War battle. It began to reflect America's evolving tradition of coastal defense. British and French threats to the security of the United States spawned the First System of Fortifications and led in stages to a new Fort Moultrie. Advances in the field of artillery contributed to the fort's stature as a bulwark of American security. Finally, a series of dramatic events ranging from the controversy over Nullification to the imprisonment of an Indian leader focused public attention from time to time on the fort.

Fresh from its victory against England, the young Nation turned from questions of military readiness to the many challenges of social and economic development. The South Carolina legislature passed a resolution in 1791 "permitting people to build on Sullivan's Island on one-half acre lots." By 1802, visitor John Lambert noted that "almost every part of the island, which is nearly three miles long, is now occupied, and contains upwards of two hundred dwelling houses besides kitchens and out offices." The little island settlement of Moultrieville was incorporated in 1817. As for Charleston itself, a medical college opened in 1822; The Citadel, a military college, was founded 20 years later. Yet along with such strides, problems of vigilance and defense could not be ignored.

British-American relations in the decades after the Revolution were, to say the least, strained. Trade between the two nations, no longer on a colony-crown basis, settled down to a commercial rivalry. British merchants still operated trading posts in Canada and the Northwest, and exerted great economic influence throughout the Great Lakes region. Americans accused Britain of instigating hostile Indian attacks on frontier settlements. When England went to war against revolutionary France in 1793, the United States carried on a neutral trade with both countries—and incurred the wrath of both. Britain and France, who had declared blockades on each other and had prohibited U.S. trade with their enemy's West Indian colonies, began to capture and condemn American ships laden with food and other valuable cargoes. The United States found itself helpless. British warships even entered and left American ports at will.

President Washington and the Congress moved to remedy these affronts. In February 1794, Secretary of War Henry Knox submitted to the House of Representatives a report on the ports and harbors of the United States requiring defense. Charleston was one of 16 such ports. Based on this study, Congress authorized what became know as the First American System of Fortifications. By June, William Moultrie, now governor of South Carolina, approved projects on Sullivans Island, at Fort Johnson, and along Charleston's Battery. Black and white workers laid the foundation for the second Fort Moultrie in early August. Construction on the fort accelerated after a British squadron appeared off the bar and, in full view of workers on Sullivans Island, boarded the American ship *Norfolk* and impressed four sailors into English service.

Meantime, President Washington had sent Chief Justice John Jay to London to reach a diplomatic

Fort Moultrie's Battle with the Sea

A large part of Fort Moultrie's history has followed the sea's turbulent course. A hurricane on the night of October 6, 1783, helped wreck the original fort. A killer storm on the evening of September 7, 1804, ravaged the second Fort Moultrie, shown in the diagram at right. A third fort of brick and masonry, below, was completed in December 1809 and helped its garrison survive the wild hurricane of August 27, 1813. Even so, flood tides rushed through the sally port and rose to a height of two and

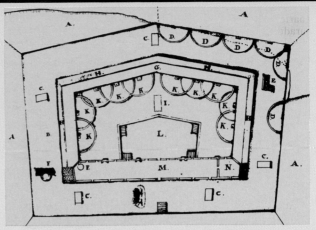

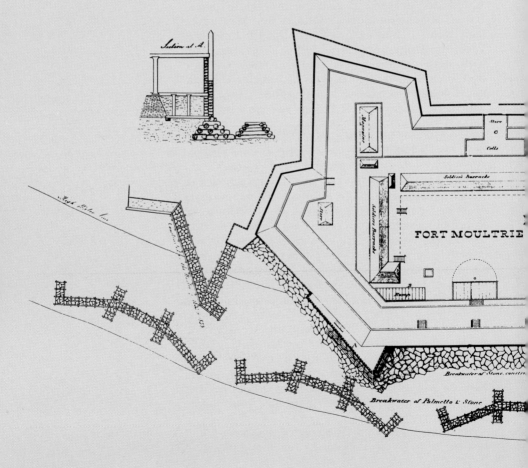

one-half feet in the officers' quarters and four feet on the parade ground. This storm killed nine civilians, demolished the island's houses, and drowned its livestock.

By 1830 the relentless sea had eaten its way toward Fort Moultrie. Eroding through beach and the rubble of the second Fort Moultrie, the surf washed at flood tide to the fort's ramparts. Moultrie's southwest angle finally crumbled in July 1831. The Army Corps of Engineers quickly embarked on a long struggle to save not only the fort but Sullivans Island itself.

After unsuccessfully trying out log and stone shielding piers, the engineers constructed an extensive and costly network of jetties and breakwaters. These obstacles, made of brush and rock-filled cribs, paralleled the channel front at various low-water lines and accumulated sand with each high water. The plan proved effective in gradually reclaiming buffer strips of beach. Periodically, the Corps repaired and strengthened their breakwaters. Repair work went on continuously, and the western third of Sullivans Island was at last salvaged from the elements. The third Fort Moultrie remained a haven for hurricane victims and stood as a symbol of triumph in its never-ending fight against the sea.

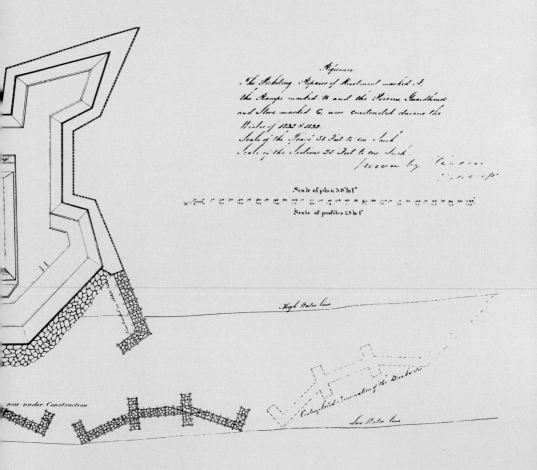

settlement. By autumn the mission proved to be a success, for the two countries signed a complex but effective agreement. Among other provisions, Britain agreed to repay American shipping losses and to evacuate its posts in the Northwest Territory in return for strict United States neutrality and American payment of pre-Revolution debts to British merchants. After ratifying the Jay Treaty in 1795, Congress became unwilling to complete the expensive coastal defense system. In January 1796 work on Fort Moultrie No. 2 "was directed to be left as it was." Only the frontal foundations, along with the bakehouse, barracks, and officers' quarters, had been completed.

But the danger had not passed. War-torn France resented the Jay Treaty and committed new depredations against American maritime commerce. In 1797 President John Adams sent to France a three-man commission, which included South Carolina's Charles Cotesworth Pinckney. The commission sought to open negotiations on an American-French commercial agreement, but France's ruling Directory refused a meeting. Three mysterious French agents (later identified as "X", "Y", and "Z" in Adams' report to Congress) finally approached the commission and suggested a $12 million loan to France (and a bribe of $240,000 to Minister of Foreign Affairs Talleyrand) as a prerequisite for opening diplomatic relations. After Congress and the country learned of this humiliating "XYZ Affair" in the spring of 1798, preparations for war began. Congress appropriated military funds, and citizens cried the slogan, "Millions for defence, but not one cent for tribute!" For the next two years, the United States waged an undeclared war with France at sea. The fledgling American navy dominated the naval war and helped convince France that the United States would not tolerate French insults. By 1800 both countries were ready to put an end to the conflict.

Throughout this volatile period, the second Fort Moultrie underwent a renaissance. Congress eventually voted $115,000 to complete the First System of Fortifications, and at a public meeting on May 5, 1798, Charlestonians agreed to raise funds to strengthen the "fortification and defence of the city and harbour of Charles Town." Much of this money helped build Castle Pinckney on Shutes Folly, an island in the inner harbor. Over $12,000 supplemented the Federal appropriation for Fort Moultrie. By November 1798 Fort Moultrie No. 2 was finished. Smaller than called for in the original 1794 plans, this five-sided enclosed fort was surrounded by a ditch eight feet deep and a glacis, or exposed slope, 50 feet wide. A half-dozen English 12-pounder cannons, along with a well and shot furnace, were positioned in the ditch. Behind these rose earth and timber walls, 17 feet high at the crest. Inside the fort were "The Place of Arms," the bombproof, a well, a brick magazine, and ten French 26-pounders. The barracks, bakehouse, and officers' quarters stood at the rear of the fort, between it and The Cove.

The life of the second Fort Moultrie was short. After 1800, military expenditures were again cut, and for the next five years the trio of Charleston Harbor forts—Moultrie, Johnson, and Pinckney—received a total of less than $50 from the Federal Government. In September 1804 these forts were all but destroyed by a fierce hurricane. The storm washed away a score of island homes and killed a young black man. In the spring of 1807 a visiting engineer sadly observed of Fort Moultrie that "there is nothing in the whole of this work that can be considered in any other view, than as heaps of rubbish . . . the guns have pitched forward; and bearing their broken carriages behind them, lie on the brick."

In 1806 the Jay Treaty expired. The British, in a life-and-death struggle with Napoleon, were in no mood to tolerate American trade with France. Again Britain intercepted American merchant ships and impressed British citizens—and some Americans—into the Royal Navy. Again America's coastal defenses "stood in need of finishing, or repairs." During the winter of 1807-8, a Second American System of Fortifications was begun, and Congress eventually appropriated $3 million for this five-year undertaking. The Second System, which included masonry forts and open batteries, was more elaborate than the First. Unlike the First System, it was constructed under the supervision of American, not foreign, engineers. Yet the old cycle of sudden threat, emergency preparations followed by long-term neglect, still had not been broken.

Maj. Gen. Alexander Macomb was a young engineer officer in charge of coastal defenses in Georgia and the Carolinas when he designed and built the third Fort Moultrie. His distinguished service in the War of 1812 won him recognition and promotion. In 1828 he was appointed commanding general of the U.S. Army, a post he held until his death 13 years later.

The Second System, however, meant permanence for Fort Moultrie. Directed by Maj. Alexander Macomb, work on the third Fort Moultrie began during the summer of 1808. Its construction required a year and a half, but the result was well worth the wait. Moultrie No. 3, enclosed by 15-foot-high brick walls, with a spacious brick magazine, 40 guns, and quarters for three companies of soldiers, presented a stout three-sided battery along the seafront. When America finally declared war on Great Britain in June 1812, many citizens in the South and West looked with confidence toward the outcome.

The War of 1812 was a kind of slow-motion replay of the Revolutionary War. Initial American attacks on Canada were repulsed, and the British mounted a sluggish counterattack. Once again the British set up a blockade, and American privateers harassed British shipping. At Charleston, Fort Moultrie's garrison, including units of the 3d and 18th U.S. Infantry, the 2d U.S. Artillery, and the South Carolina militia, cheered as privateers like *Wasp* successfully ran the blockade and captured foreign cargoes. The 170-ton *Saucy Jack,* perhaps the first Charleston-built privateer of the war, wrought havoc with enemy commerce and took many prizes, among them the British ship *Pelham.*

Fort Moultrie's contact with the war was indirect, a series of minor events against the backdrop of blockade and the sails of lurking British warships. In April 1813, the revenue cutter *Gallatin* blew up in Charleston Harbor and the body of a seaman killed in the explosion was taken to the fort for an inquest. Moultrie fired its cannon in celebration of American victories at Lake Erie and elsewhere. Even in wartime, duty at Fort Moultrie was tedious. The long watches, the daily drills at cannon and battalion exercises, the rare furloughs and severe discipline—these were not the qualities of luxury or excitement. The peace signed on Christmas Eve 1814 came as a relief to both sides. The Treaty of Ghent reflected the stalemate of the war. It resolved no fundamental issues, but merely stopped the fighting.

Although Americans could look back with pride to victories at Lake Champlain and New Orleans, there were also bitter memories, such as the British burning of Washington, D.C. Lingering suspicion and hostility provided the impetus for a new stage of

American coastal defense, a system which, in the words of military historian Emanuel R. Lewis, would elevate "seacoast fortification from the status of an emergency measure to a position of foremost importance among the nation's major methods of defense." Construction of the Third System forts, of which Sumter and Pulaski are good examples, began in 1817 and continued until the Civil War. Characterized by more powerful cannon and heavily armed and tiered forts of thick masonry, this system represented a considerable advance in basic notions of coastal and harbor security.

Although the Third System forts received most of the attention and money during the years before the Civil War, Fort Moultrie was maintained and periodically strengthened into an important national military post. Among the additional structures built were a hospital, kitchens, barracks, workshops, and storehouses. When the United States went to war with Mexico in 1846, Fort Moultrie served as a staging area for companies of the 3d U.S. Artillery, the 12th and 13th U.S. Infantry, the 3d U.S. Dragoons, and other regiments. Later, while Fort Sumter neared completion in Charleston Harbor, soldiers from Fort Moultrie stood guard at the manmade island on which it stood.

In the last years of the 1820s and early 1830s one of the most severe crises in American history threatened to divide the Union and provided for Fort Moultrie an intense interval. In 1828 Congress passed a high tariff designed to protect the infant northern industries. This "Tariff of Abominations," as Southerners called it, infuriated many South Carolina citizens, including Senator John C. Calhoun, for it protected northern manufacturers much more than it did the raw materials, particularly rice and cotton, produced by Southern planters. South Carolinians felt this amounted to a tax on the South for the profit of the North. The tariff also raised the possibility of retaliation by foreign countries, which could devastate planters dependent upon the heavy export of their products. Even more important was the veiled implication that if Congress could pass an unconstitutional protective tariff harmful to Southern interests, it could also legislate against the South's "peculiar institution"—slavery.

Rising to these threats, Calhoun published in 1828

"The South Carolina Exposition and Protest" in which he formulated the idea of "state interposition." He maintained that if the Federal Government should pass a law harmful to an individual State, then an elected convention from that State could interpose its will between the Federal Government and the people as a whole, thus nullifying any effect of the oppressive law.

In 1832 South Carolinians had cause to test Calhoun's theory. That summer Congress passed a new tariff designed to correct the abuses of the 1828 tariff, but it did not significantly reduce the earlier duties. Incensed South Carolinians voted the States' rights party to overwhelming victory in the autumn elections. The party quickly planned a rebellious convention for late November. Alexander Macomb, commander of the Army, alerted Charleston's garrisons, including the one at Fort Moultrie, "to be vigilant" against a possible effort "to surprize, seize, and occupy" the forts. Maj. Gen. Winfield Scott was ordered to Charleston, along with several companies of artillery. By the end of the year, nine artillery companies—almost a quarter of all in the Army—garrisoned Fort Moultrie; two more occupied Castle Pinckney.

On November 24 the South Carolina convention declared the tariffs of 1828 and 1832 unconstitutional and announced that these laws would become null and void in the State on February 1, 1833. If the U.S. Government tried to stop them, they said, South Carolina would secede from the Union. In a proclamation, President Andrew Jackson denounced this doctrine of nullification, but the *Charleston Mercury* warned: "Any attempt at coercion on the part of the President, as it would be totally illegal, would be repelled by force, and perhaps lead to consequences, personal to himself of which he little dreams." Undaunted, Jackson backed a "Force Bill" in Congress that would allow him to use military force in the situation. South Carolina's governor, Robert Y. Hayne, reacted by calling for 10,000 State militiamen. At Fort Moultrie, Capt. William Eliason and a 40-man crew buttressed the fortification with an eight-foot palisade and shielded gunmounts. One soldier wrote home: *We hardly know whether it is war or peace. We are, however, prepared for the worst. We have got a stout picketing round the work, our cannons are mounted, muskets loaded and all in such order that we will not be taken in a hurry. If the rascals do intend to keep on in their iniquitous course their first step must be to attack this fort as it is a key which completely locks up nullification. Without this fort, the "nullies" can do nothing. . . .*

Charlestonians delayed taking decisive action until the tariff actually went into effect. One prominent gentleman agreed not to bring his cargo of Cuban sugar through customs until the proper time, but he knew that if collision were finally necessary, "his fellow citizens would go even to the death with him for his sugar." The tension built by such rhetoric subsided a bit in mid-February when soldiers from Fort Moultrie and Castle Pinckney were sent into downtown Charleston to fight a spreading fire. The artillerists nearly clashed with militia, but someone called out that "they had come over to go to the death with them for their sugar." Both sides laughed, put out the fire, and were congratulated by local newspapers.

As it turned out, this happy incident was a prelude to conciliation. South Carolina found that a secession move would not be supported by other Southern States. One reason for this lay in the fact that Jackson had placated States like Georgia, Mississippi, and Alabama by strongly advocating Indian removal. (Ironically, the President flouted Federal law in the case of the Indians, but when confronted with South Carolina's nullification attempts, he determined to use force to quell the revolt.) Kentucky's less emotional Henry Clay defused the Force Act of March 1 by hammering out a compromise tariff, which Jackson signed the same day. The crisis passed, and Fort Moultrie's expanded garrison dwindled, but this "rehearsal" for secession was not soon forgotten.

Throughout the early 1800s general improvements in artillery helped modernize the armament of Fort Moultrie and similar coastal fortifications. In the Revolutionary War, American artillery had gone through a slow and painful birth, using for the most part random French and British pieces. These ranged from basic, flat-trajectory, long-range guns to howitzers which had a shorter range but could fire shot or shell, to mortars with their high-angle fire. The size of most pre-Civil War guns, which fired solid

As lieutenants and captains, these six officers served together at Fort Moultrie in 1843. Clockwise from upper left: John F. Reynolds, Erasmus D. Keyes, William T. Sherman, Braxton Bragg, Thomas W. Sherman (often referred to as "the other Sherman" but no relation to William T.), and George H. Thomas. All later became generals and won fame in the Civil War.

spherical shot, was measured by the weight of the ball and referred to as "pounders" of various numbers. The size of mortars and howitzers, which fired shells of varying weight, was usually given as the inside diameter of the bore in inches.

At the end of the War of 1812, the new-found American artillery industry relied for its coastal defense on pieces like 18-, 24-, and 32-pounder guns, 8-inch howitzers, and 10-inch mortars. In 1819 the U.S. Army began producing cannon on a larger, more systematic scale. Many of the guns made in America were called "columbiads," a term derived possibly from Joel Barlow's patriotic poem "The Columbiad," published in 1809. During the 1840s columbiad came to mean an 8- or 10-inch gun of great range and flexibility. By the mid-1800s American garrison pieces included such reliables as 32- and 42-pounders, 8- and 10-inch howitzers, and 10- and 13-inch mortars. In November 1860, on the eve of the Civil War, Fort Moultrie's armament consisted of over 50 cannon: nineteen 32-pounders, sixteen 24-pounders, ten 8-inch columbiads, six howitzers for flank defense, four bronze 6-pounders, and one 10-inch mortar.

The men who oversaw such weapons at Fort Moultrie led a difficult garrison life during the years between the War of 1812 and the Civil War. They drilled constantly on the large guns, usually without being allowed to fire valuable powder or shot. Maintenance of the heavy ordnance against salt and humidity presented a great problem. Although no soldier died in combat during these years, disease took a huge toll. A yellow fever epidemic killed half the garrison, while malaria continued to torment the entire Low Country area. Confronted by such hardship and boredom, many of the men turned to liquor for comfort and excitement. Fire struck the fort in October 1822 and destroyed the officers quarters, which were rebuilt the following year. The number of privates averaged 50 per company, and each was paid $6 a month. To discourage desertion, $1 of this monthly pay was withheld from each new private. If at the end of two years he had "honestly and faithfully" served, he received a lump sum of $24.

Life for the officers at Fort Moultrie could be highly desirable. Gen. William T. Sherman wrote of the fort in his *Memoirs:* "Our life there was of strict

Short-story writer Edgar Allen Poe served at Fort Moultrie as a private in Company H, 1st U.S. Artillery, from November 1827 to the end of 1828. He used Sullivans Island as the setting for several of his stories.

garrison duty, with plenty of leisure for hunting and social entertainments." Sherman even took up painting in 1842. It was rumored that Lt. Braxton Bragg relieved his boredom by writing memoranda to himself; as quartermaster, for instance, he would complain of bad beef to Bragg-the-commander. In 1843 there were a half-dozen lieutenants and captains at the post who would later become generals: William T. Sherman, Bragg, John F. Reynolds, Thomas W. Sherman, Erasmus D. Keyes, and George H. Thomas.

Although the fort's routine varied little from year to year, individuality did not disappear. Edgar Allen Poe, famous poet and writer of ingenious short stories, spent over a year at Fort Moultrie. In 1827, young Poe left his foster father and in Boston enlisted for five years in company H of the 1st U.S. Artillery. He signed his name "Edgar Allen Perry." A recruiter added four years to his age and entered him as 22 years old. In November, Company H was transferred from Massachusetts to Fort Moultrie, and the literate "Private Perry" landed a job as commissary clerk. The next summer, a few months before Company H moved on to Virginia's Fort Monroe, Poe was promoted to the job of artificer (weapons repairman).

While stationed at Fort Moultrie, Poe made good use of his time. He began to write his longest poem, "Al Aaraaf," here and gathered material for later stories. "The Gold Bug," an intricate tale of pirate treasure, depends greatly on its Sullivans Island setting: *This island is a very singular one. It consists of little else than the sea sand, and is about three miles long. Its breadth at no point exceeds a quarter of a mile. It is separated from the mainland by a scarcely perceptible creek, oozing its way through a wilderness of reeds and slime, a favorite resort of the marsh hen. The vegetation, as might be supposed, is scant, or at least dwarfish. No trees of any magnitude are to be seen. Near the western extremity, where Fort Moultrie stands . . . may be found, indeed, the bristly palmetto; but the whole island, with the exception of this western point, and a line of hard, white beach on the seacoast, is covered with a dense undergrowth of the sweet myrtle so much prized by the horticulturists of England. The shrub here often attains the heights of fifteen or twenty feet, and forms an almost impenetrable coppice, burdening the air with its fragrance.*

Poe also mentions Fort Moultrie at the end of his story "The Balloon Hoax," in which eight passengers aboard the balloon *Victoria* have allegedly crossed the Atlantic in 75 hours: *It was nearly dead calm when the voyagers first came in view of the coast, which was immediately recognized by both the seamen, and by Mr. Osborne. The latter gentleman having acquaintances at Fort Moultrie, it was immediately resolved to descend in its vicinity. The balloon was brought over the beach (the tide being out and the sand hard, smooth, and admirably adapted for a descent), and the grapnel let go, which took firm hold at once. The inhabitants of the island, and of the fort, thronged out, of course, to see the balloon. . . . The balloon was exhausted and secured without trouble; and when the MS. from which this narrative is compiled was dispatched from Charleston, the party were still at Fort Moultrie.*

Another break in the tedium of post life came a decade later, when the Seminole war leader Osceola was captured by American forces and taken to Fort Moultrie in January 1838. He was confined here only a few weeks before he died from quinsy, a severe throat infection. Throughout his captivity Osceola received courteous treatment and even became a local celebrity. At the fort, he sometimes made fun of the U.S. Army's "mode of warfare, and gave an excellent pantomime . . . of the manner of the white man and the Indian loading and firing." Osceola was "at liberty within the walls, and roamed about at pleasure," and many Charlestonians took the opportunity to visit him. On January 6 Osceola and four Seminole chiefs attended Charleston's New Theatre production of "Honey Moon." The event inspired a five-verse poem entitled "Osceola at the Charleston Theatre." When Osceola died, the garrison at Fort Moultrie buried him with military honors near the fort entrance.

Seminole Indian leader Osceola vigorously opposed U.S. Government efforts to remove his people from their ancestral lands. His two-year resistance ended with his arrest in October 1837. He was confined at Fort Moultrie in January 1838 and died there several weeks later.

Poetry and war, sickness and turmoil, rebuilding and security: these themes and a host of events and details helped define the years at Fort Moultrie between the American Revolution and the Civil War. But as the fateful decade of the 1860s drew near, these myriad hues divided into clashing standards of blue and gray.

HARPER'S WEEKLY.

A JOURNAL OF CIVILIZATION.

Vol. V.—No. 221.]   NEW YORK, SATURDAY, MARCH 23, 1861.   [Price Five Cents.

Entered according to Act of Congress, in the Year 1861, by Harper & Brothers, in the Clerk's Office of the District Court for the Southern District of New York.

SUMTER.

Capt. T. Seymour. ☆ 2d Lieut. G. W. Snyder. ☆ 1st Lt. J. C. Davis. ☆ 2d Lt. R. K. Meade. ☆ 1st Lt. T. Talbot.

Capt. A. Doubleday. ☆ Maj. R. Anderson. ☆ Asst. Surg. S. W. Crawford. ☆ Capt. J. G. Foster.

MAJOR ANDERSON'S COMMAND AT FORT SUMTER.—From a Photograph taken in the Fort.—[See Page 190.]

evacuate Moultrie and move to Fort Sumter. This secret maneuver was accomplished on the evening of December 26: "Every thing being in readiness, we passed out of the main gates, and silently made our way for about a quarter of a mile to a spot where the boats were hidden behind an irregular pile of rocks." Anderson's men easily occupied Sumter, for only a party of workman was on the island.

A rear guard had been left at Moultrie to man five cannon in case South Carolina guard boats attempted to interfere with the crossing. This rear guard was soon joined by a small detachment that returned to destroy the guns. The wooden carriages of ten columbiads were set afire; the remaining cannon were "spiked," rendering them useless. By the time South Carolina troops entered Fort Moultrie late the next day, the fort had been temporarily crippled. Fort Sumter lay in Union hands. A new year—and a new chapter in the history of Moultrie and the United States—was about to begin.

Through the next three months the opposing lines were tightened. A half-dozen other Southern States seceded, drew up a constitution in Montgomery, Alabama, and formed the Confederate States of America. Col. Roswell Ripley, commander of the 1st South Carolina Artillery Battalion at Fort Moultrie, further strengthened Moultrie's defenses. Hundreds of blacks labored to construct traverses to shield the officers' quarters and screen guns on the fort's seaward front. Besides building a steep parapet of earth on the southwest side, Ripley's men protected other gun emplacements with "high and solid merlons, formed of timber, sandbags, and earth, raised between them." Fort Moultrie now had 30 guns, of which eleven—8-inch columbiads and 24- and 32-pounders—pointed toward Sumter.

The first test of this armament came in April 1861. Fort Sumter stuck like a thorn in the side of the South, and the Confederacy was determined to remove that thorn. At 4:30 on the morning of April 12, a shot from Fort Johnson—the shot that started the war—signalled the Confederate batteries to begin firing. Two hours later, Sumter replied by shooting twice at the angled walls of Moultrie, but the balls glanced harmlessly off the bricks. Southern firing continued unabated, and by evening Sumter replied in full measure against Moultrie and nearby batteries on Sullivans Island. At the end of this first fierce day, reports came back to the eagerly waiting citizens of Charleston: *The advantage was unquestionably upon the side of Fort Moultrie. In that fort not a gun was dismounted, not a wound received, not the slightest permanent injury sustained by any of its defences, while every ball from Fort Moultrie left its mark upon Fort Sumter. . . . The last two or three hours before dark, Major Anderson devoted himself exclusively to Fort Moultrie, and the two fortresses had a grand duello. Game to the last, though much more exposed, Fort Moultrie held her own, and, it is believed, a little more than her own. Towards night, several rounds of red-hot shot were thrown into the barracks of the enemy. . . .*

The firing of hot shot was risky. The gun crew first had to place a divider, such as sod or wet hay, between the powder and the heated ball. The men then had to fire the shot as soon as possible to lessen the chance of an accident. Moultrie's artillery crews accomplished this successfully and gave Sumter's garrison fits. In retaliation, Doubleday, at Sumter, aimed a 42-pounder toward the elegant Moultrie House Hotel on Sullivans Island and let loose a tremendous charge against the second story of the building. It was a direct hit. Reported a newsman: "A party of gentlemen were sitting in the parlor, watching the fight. The gentlemen scattered miscellaneously." When asked later about his choice of target, Doubleday replied that the hotel had never given him good room service in earlier, more peaceful days.

On the second and last day of the bombardment, Fort Moultrie and the Confederate guns ringing Sumter began firing in the early morning and poured shot and shell across the harbor for several hours. By noon, Sumter's barracks and officers' quarters were burning out of control. Smoke and fire raged throughout the fort until, in the early afternoon, onlookers saw a white flag on the ramparts. Sumter had surrendered. Amazingly, no one on either side had been killed. Moultrie suffered four casualties, however, along with extensive damage to the barracks, officers' quarters, and shot furnace.

Over the next two years, the Union maintained a blockade of Charleston. As in the War of 1812, ships attempted to evade the blockade and to collect

much-needed supplies as well as healthy profits. One Union sailor described such maneuverings: *A shrewd blockade-running captain could steal in close to the shore of Sullivans Island a few miles up the coast, then by hugging the shore dangerously close (in which he would be aided by a few signal lights flashed from the shore) he could succeed in running past the vessels blockading the northern (or Sullivans Island) channel and edging past the monitors picketing the main channel. ... The blockade runners did not always succeed in getting by, as an occasional burning wreck to be seen on the shore of Sullivans Island attested.*

Meanwhile, the Confederates strengthened and extended Charleston's defenses, concentrating largely on Sullivans and Morris Islands. Two batteries—Bee and Beauregard—flanked Moultrie, and Battery Marshall protected Breach Inlet to the north. Complete with magazines and bomb-proofs, these works were solidly made of sand covered with sod. The 1st South Carolina Infantry moved in to man the island's guns.

Their first test came in the spring of 1863, when Rear Adm. Samuel F. Du Pont tried to force his way into Charleston Harbor with nine Federal ironclads, including Du Pont's flagship *New Ironsides.* At 2:30 on the afternoon of April 7, the ships began a slow, single-file advance up the main channel. Thirty minutes later they came within range of Confederate guns at Sumter and Moultrie. Fort Moultrie concentrated its fire on the monitor *Weehawken,* whose iron siding proved an effective shield against the 53 hits from the forts. But these tank-like ships were also unwieldy and uncertain in unfamiliar waters. After several hours of furious fighting, *New Ironsides* retreated from the range of Moultrie's guns, followed by the other ironclads. *Keokuk,* with 90 hits, sank the next day off Morris Island. The Confederates at Charleston had won their initial battle with the U.S. Navy.

The defenders of Charleston Harbor wasted no time in improving their positions. Three huge 10-inch columbiads arrived to supplement Fort Moultrie's 8-inch columbiads, 24- and 32-pounders, and two 10-inch mortars in the nearby outworks. Batteries Bee and Beauregard were extended all the way to the fort, creating two intermediate works known as

Gen P.G.T. Beauregard, who directed the Confederate bombardment of Fort Sumter, had studied artillery under Major Anderson at West Point, **Left, top:** *These heavy cannon, photographed at Fort Moultrie four days after the battle, took part in the attack on Sumter.* **Bottom:** *This map shows the Union and Confederate batteries ringing Charleston Harbor in 1863. In mid-September of that year heavy Union guns on Morris Island and in the marshes to the west began to hurl shells into Charleston and Forts Sumter and Moultrie.*

"In the Summer of 1863. . . ."

Throughout the Civil War, an infinite variety of men and women kept personal accounts of trials endured, memories saved. From general to private, from the wealthy to the indigent, thousands wrote individual chronicles that help form a broad portrait of a nation at war with itself.

In 1879 Jacob Stroyer, shown at right, published his memoir of the war, called *My Life in the South*. He wrote eloquently of such scenes as Union monitors floating near Charleston Harbor "like a flock of black sheep feeding on a plain of grass." Stroyer's memory for detail allowed him to explain small events in terms of their wider meaning. Yet there was another element that made Stroyer's *Life* compelling reading, for Jacob Stroyer was a black man and, in 1863, a slave:

"In the summer of 1863 with thousands of other negroes, gathered from the various parts of the state, I was freighted to the city of Charleston, South Carolina, and the group in which my lot fell was sent to Sullivan's Island. . . . Our work was to repair forts [like Battery Rutledge, below, painted by Charleston artist Conrad Chapman], build batteries, mount guns, and arrange them. While the men were engaged at such work, the boys of my age, namely, thirteen, and some older, waited on officers and carried water for the men at work, and in general acted as messengers between different points on the island. . . .

"We fared better on these fortifications than we had

at home on the plantations. This was the case at least with those of us who were on Sullivan's Island. Our work in general on the fortifications was not hard, we had a great deal of spare time, and although we knew that our work in the Confederate service was against our liberty, yet we were delighted to be in military service.

"We felt an exalted pride that, having spent a little time at these war points, we had gained some knowledge which would put us beyond our fellow negroes at home on the plantations, while they would increase our pride by crediting us with far more knowledge than it was possible for us to have gained. . . .

"The change from the cabins and from the labor on the old plantations so filled our cup of joy that we were sorry when the two months of our stay on the island was ended."

Batteries Marion and Rutledge. Four separate two-gun batteries, plus New Battery at Cove Inlet, rounded out the Sullivans Island defenses. In August Gen. P.G.T. Beauregard ordered a good portion of Moultrie's barracks and officers' quarters demolished. Additional sandbags and protective traverses helped convert Fort Moultrie from the usual masonry structure into a "powerful earthwork."

As a result, Rear Adm. John A. Dahlgren's attempts to take Sumter on September 1 and 2, and again on the 7th and 8th, met with stiff opposition. On the evening of the 7th *Weehawken* attempted to navigate the narrow channel between Fort Sumter and Morris Island, but it grounded. The next morning six ironclads engaged Fort Moultrie and the other land batteries in a second major duel. Moultrie fired away at *Weehawken* and *New Ironsides,* yet these two ships valiantly accounted for themselves. A 15-inch shell from *Weehawken* detonated an ammunition stack near one of Moultrie's 8-inch columbiads, killing 16 gunners. Shot and shell from *New Ironsides* smashed against the remaining sections of Moultrie's quarters and hurled "fragments of every description in every direction, rendering it almost impossible to pass from one portion of the fort to another." Yet the Navy, also under heavy fire, soon had enough. When *Weehawken* was refloated in mid-afternoon, the Union ironclads withdrew. "A lot of houses burning near and back of Moultrie," wrote a sailor aboard *Nahant.* "Went in again to help protect *Weehawken;* she had got off; we fired both guns at Moultrie for spite."

A day later, on September 8, Fort Moultrie's artillery helped to defeat a small-boat assault on Fort Sumter. Moultrie "fired like a devil," and in a matter of minutes the Union lost five boats and 124 men killed, wounded, or captured. In November a third confrontation between Fort Moultrie and the ironclads ended with casualties on both sides. During these and later months, work continued on defenses to shield Moultrie from both naval assaults and Union guns emplaced on the northern end of Morris Island. In the war's final years Charleston Harbor became a terrifying scene of constant bombardment.

By early 1865 the outcome of the Civil War was certain. Sherman's army embarked on its final trek northward from Savannah into South Carolina. In

The rapid advance of Gen. William T. Sherman's army north from Savannah in February 1865 forced the Confederates to abandon Charleston and the harbor forts. Four years of war and 18 months of sustained bombardment had substantially altered Moultrie's appearance and U.S. engineers were faced with a problem of what to do with it and the other fortifications that once defended Charleston Harbor. These photographs, taken shortly after Federal troops reoccupied the work, show (top to bottom) Moultrie's half-demolished sally port, the fort's interior and nearby mortar batteries bearing on the sea approaches to the harbor, and the battered hot-shot furnace.

53

February the inevitable took place. In the cool evening air of the 17th the Southerners abandoned Fort Moultrie and Sullivans Island. On the following morning members of the 3d Rhode Island Heavy Artillery crossed the parapets of Fort Moultrie and raised the United States flag. War had ended in Charleston Harbor, but men and women alike would long remember these bloody years.

Following the war, the Army Corps of Engineers reevaluated the expensive masonry fortifications of the Second and Third Systems and found them to be obsolete. There were two main reasons for this. First, naval development—the introduction of steam power in ironclad warships—had increased tactical mobility and rendered fixed shore positions less awesome to modern warships. Second, and equally important, revolutionary improvements in artillery and ammunition had made it possible for navies to wreck these stately masonry forts with near impunity. The heart of this advance in weaponry was clearly embodied in the new rifled cannon.

Artillerists had long recognized the possibility of achieving for cannon the accuracy of rifled small arms. By cutting a series of twisting grooves inside the gun's barrel, hunters and riflemen had for years shot further and more precisely. The problem for artillery was developing a projectile which "could be loaded easily yet fit the bore tightly enough in firing to take the spin imparted by . . . the rifling." In the 1850s, large caliber projectiles began to be perfected. Most worked on the principle of expansion, which allowed them to be easily loaded. Upon firing, projectiles like the Reed, Burton, Dyer, and Mullane expanded at their soft-metal base. The Hotchkiss, frequently used in Union guns, worked by forcing together two iron pieces and spreading out the lead between them. Such effective ammunition permitted larger rifles on the order of Charles James' converted bronze smoothbores. Yet the bronze on these wore down quickly, and artillerists in general recognized the need for new rifled tubes.

Robert Parrott, supervisor of the West Point Foundry, had been developing such a design during the 1850s. In 1861 he received a patent for a rifled cannon made of cast iron and reinforced at the breech with a wrought-iron band. The Parrott and the sleek, tough, wrought-iron Ordnance Rifles became standard weaponry in 1861 and were supplemented by the English Blakely, the Armstrong, the Whitworth, and other contemporary pieces. These guns had bores ranging from 2.75 to 12.75 inches in diameter and included the huge 200- and 300-pounder Parrotts. Rifles came to be widely used during the later years of the Civil War. In 1864, for example, Fort Moultrie's armament consisted of five 10-inch smoothbore columbiads, two 24-pounder smoothbores, two 8-inch rifles, and one rifled 32-pounder.

One byproduct of the rifling revolution helped spell doom for masonry fort walls. This advance came in the form of a new type of fuse. Armed with the knowledge that a spinning projectile would always hit its target at the same end, weapons experts rushed to devise a fuse which would detonate the shell upon impact. Charles James, Robert Parrott, and a host of others produced variations on a plunger-type detonator.

These innovations persuaded the Corps of Engineers and Congress that post-war fortifications would have to differ radically from earlier systems. By the time Congress passed a Fortifications Bill in March 1871, concepts of coastal defense had undergone a transformation. Batteries, offering versatility and decentralization, were now considered basic elements of defense. Gun emplacements were enlarged and set on platforms of granite or concrete. Well-protected ammunition rooms with magazines stood behind thick buffers of earth and concrete.

At Moultrie, like many projects dependent on public financing, the modernization of the fort proceeded spasmodically. Despite layoffs and lengthy work stoppages over the next four years, laborers removed sand, salvaged brick, and poured concrete foundations for magazines and gun platforms. The sally port was rebuilt, along with flanking guardrooms and bombproofs. Two huge 15-inch Rodmans and two 200-pounder Parrotts were mounted inside the rebuilt fortification, plus four 13-inch mortars north of the fort.

When work on Moultrie finally ended in 1876, this and similar projects remained short of completion. Compared with former appropriations for seacoast defense, the program of the 1870s was poorly funded. Yet new tactical patterns had been set. America was about to enter the modern era of coastal defense.

The Story of the Rodman

About the same time that rifled artillery was coming into use in the United States, another advance in weaponry was taking place which represented the ultimate achievement of the smooth-bore tradition. The man responsible for this development was Thomas J. Rodman, right, a career ordnance officer who had been conducting experiments in gun casting and construction since his graduation from West Point in 1841.

Rodman's early investigations convinced him that

many structural flaws in artillery were due to the process of cooling the newly cast gun from the outside in. The stresses at firing began at the bore, the exact point where cannon were weakest. To remedy this, he devised a way to make a casting which solidified from the inside out. In 1847 he obtained a patent for his idea and tried it out by circulating air through the core of a mold kept hot with a surrounding fire. The technique worked; later he used water instead of air.

Over the next decade he slowly proved the new process by a series of tedious experiments. In 1851, for example, two 8-inch columbiads—one made from the older solid casts, the other hollow-cast—were tested together. The solid 8-incher burst after 73 firings; the Rodman never burst, even after 1,500 rounds.

But Rodman was still not satisfied. "His mind," a friend wrote, "was not of that brilliant order which startles by its flashes . . . but was of that slower, more deliberate kind

which proceeds step by step, examining well each position taken before advancing to the next. When the conclusion is reached, the ground has been so closely reasoned and so firmly established that it is not lightly shaken." Rodman painstakingly improved the design for his new gun, equalizing pressures all along its length. He also reduced the sometimes excessive pressure from gunpowder by increasing the diameter of the grains and developing his "Mammoth Powder."

The results of such labor were of course the Rodmans, superior guns of 8-, 10-, 15-, and even 20-inch diameter. With this amazing smoothbore, a 15-inch version of which is shown in the photograph below, a beautiful and simple form meshed perfectly with its function. Rodmans were used during the Civil War and, in some cases, into the 20th century. Two are mounted at Fort Moultrie.

The Modern Era

After the construction of the 1870s, Fort Moultrie was placed in the hands of a fort keeper and an ordnance-sergeant. Even at this early date, visitors were beginning to tour the historic fort, yet funds were lacking for even the most minor maintenance. By 1879 weeds grew "luxuriously throughout [its] interior." An 1887 Corps of Engineers report noted the need for sodding some of the gun positions and replacing rotten doors, floors, and platforms.

Although America was at peace during these years, a movement was building for renewed attention to coastal fortifications. European powers were developing battleships with central, armored turrets and massive guns, posing an ominous threat to the shoreline defense of the United States. At the same time, American ordnance experts had been perfecting new tools with which to combat an enemy. Nitroglycerin-based powder was replacing the old black powder, and steel, breech-loading rifles were preempting the muzzle-loaders of the past. Historian Emanuel R. Lewis has observed that when compared to the 15-inch Rodmans—the ultimate cannon of old—"the new weapons which began to emerge from the developmental stage around 1890 could fire projectiles that, caliber for caliber, were four times as heavy to effective ranges two to three times as great; and they could do so with remarkably increased armor penetrating ability and accuracy."

Of significance to this trend was the development of the "disappearing" rifle. Seacoast guns mounted *en barbette* (firing over a protective wall) had long been mounted on movable wood or iron carriages. Most carriages absorbed the gun's recoil through friction as it slid back up an inclined plane. The problem with this was that it left the gun and its crew exposed. Then two American officers, Adelbert Buffington and William Crozier, perfected an experimental European design. They developed a carriage which, upon firing, effectively used the energy of recoil to lower the gun behind a protective shield. Another advantage of this disappearing rifle was its convenience for loading: shot trucks could bring unwieldy ammunition directly from the magazine to the breech of the lowered weapon.

In 1885 President Grover Cleveland appointed Secretary of War William C. Endicott to head a board that would recommend improvements for

America's coastal defense. The Endicott Board suggested arming 29 locations with mortars, powerful rifles, numerous batteries, and mines. It was not until a decade later, however, that work on this system began at Sullivans Island. By 1897 tension between the United States and Spain, aroused by the American "Yellow Press" on behalf of Cuba, had spurred construction on the entire Endicott System, including emplacements at Charleston Harbor. In February 1898 the U.S. battleship *Maine* blew up in Havana Harbor; two months later the United States declared war on Spain.

Soldiers of the 1st U.S. Artillery had returned in October 1897 to garrison Fort Moultrie. Elsewhere on Sullivans Island, Batteries Capron and Jasper received close attention. Sixteen powerful 12-inch mortars at Capron were grouped to lob their 700-pound shells simultaneously on warships. Four 10-inch disappearing rifles at massive Battery Jasper could hurl 571-pound projectiles more than eight miles. Tugboats laid electrically controlled mines in the harbor. Two 4.7-inch British Armstrong rapid-fire guns scheduled for Battery Bingham, under construction on Moultrie's southeast front, were intended to protect the minefield against sweepers. The fort's garrison even remounted two 15-inch Rodmans. Throughout May and June 1898 Charlestonians anxiously awaited the powerful fleet of Adm. Pasquale Cervera. No encounter took place, and on August 12 the "splendid little war" between the United States and Spain ended.

Two months later the Armstrongs were emplaced in Battery Bingham. The next year another reinforced concrete battery was finished at Fort Moultrie. Designated Battery McCorkle, it mounted three rapid-fire 15-pounders. In the following years, engineers built at Moultrie a mining casemate for the control of the minefield, and installed Battery Lord, equipped with another pair of 15-pounders. By 1906 four more batteries rounded out the highly versatile Endicott defenses of Charleston Harbor. Battery Huger, at Fort Sumter, contained two 12-inch rifles. Battery Logan, near Jasper, mounted a 6-inch barbette rifle and one 6-inch disappearing rifle. Batteries Thomson and Gadsden, a mile north of Logan, were armed, respectively, with two 10-inch disappearing rifles and four 6-inchers on pedestal mounts.

The Disappearing Rifle

Weapons technology advanced with great strides in the 19th century, and each advance stimulated an opposing defensive move. The disappearing rifle, developed in the 1890s, was one such example.

The increased accuracy and range of shipboard guns exposed harbor defense crews to devastating fire. A partial answer to crew protection was found in breech loading: placing shell and powder into the gun from the back. The advantage of this method over muzzle-loading

had long been recognized, but the technological problems of containing tremendous gas pressure and heat, while still being able to open and close the breach, were not overcome until after the Civil War.

A workable breech-loading mechanism permitted the development of a new carriage that would "disappear" during loading, thus protecting the men serving the guns. The development of this carriage began in Europe, but two Americans—Adelbert R. Buffington and William

Crozier—perfected the design.

The Americans replaced the hydropneumatic system of the European models with a simpler and more reliable counterweight. The gun tube was mounted at one end of a long pivot arm. At the other end, in the 10-inch model shown below mounted at Battery Thomson a mile east of Moultrie, was a 55-ton lead weight. When the gun was fired, recoil moved the tube back and down and raised the weight. At the end of the recoil, the gun locked in

position for loading. One advantage of the Buffington-Crozier carriage was that, regardless of the angle of the firing, the gun recoiled to the same position, making loading easy.

The shell was wheeled to the breech on a small carriage. The crew then rammed the projectile into position. At the command "In Battery Trip," the locking mechanism was released and the counterweight lifted the gun into firing position. Well-trained crews could fire as many as two rounds a minute.

Protected by 50 feet of earth and concrete from the flat trajectory fire of the late 19th-century warships, the disappearing rifle was nearly invulnerable. By 1916 seven of every eight heavy seacoast guns were of this type. But as it was a child of technology so it was doomed by technology. About the time of World War I a change in the design of battleship turrets permitted their guns to fire at higher angles. This gave ship guns increased range and projectiles a plunging instead of a flat trajec-

tory. A plunging fire nullified the advantages of the disappearing rifle, for the shell could reach over and behind the protective earth and concrete embankments. For protection, guns soon moved underground. The disappearing rifle was obsolete.

The modernization of America's coastal fortifications paralleled a reevaluation of the Army and Navy. In 1901 Congress divided the Army into 30 regiments of infantry, 15 cavalry regiments, and one artillery corps. The corps of artillery was divided equally into field artillery and seacoast artillery, thereby recognizing the latter as "a distinct branch of service." Also about this time, American leaders were adopting views published in 1890 by Navy Capt. Alfred Thayer Mahan, whose seminal book *The Influence of Sea Power Upon History, 1660-1783* had shown that command of the sea was a great strategic advantage. President Theodore Roosevelt especially took Mahan's philosophy to heart and emphasized the need for a strong, mobile fleet, freed by well-armed, secure seacoast fortifications from the necessity of protecting coastal areas. Little wonder it was, then, that during the first decades of this century Fort Moultrie's garrison grew to include hundreds of men and dozens of structures.

Garrison life throughout these years moved at a fairly constant pace. The day began before 6 a.m. and proceeded through breakfast, inspection, physical exercises, and company drill. After 1 p.m. the men carried out fatigue details for three hours, gun drills for an hour and a half. Taps sounded at 11 p.m. Disease still plagued the fort. In the autumn of 1918 influenza ravaged America's training camps, killing many soldiers in the South and many more in the North. Officers took meals at the island's fine boarding houses. A street car operation extended from Moultrieville all the way to The Breach. And the 1st Coast Artillery Band played at many parades and summer concerts. Mrs. Lydia Fromberger, daughter of Fort Moultrie's YMCA director at the time, later recalled this "heritage of music" along with other aspects of life at the post: *"Do you remember the wonderful smell of fresh bread as one passed the bakery; and going to the commissary ... how high and narrow the steps and porch were leading to the door. ... Then target practice, the towing of the target in the channel in front of Ft. Moultrie. Sometimes they used sub-caliber guns, sometimes the 10 and 12 inch guns and again sometimes the heavy mortar batteries. Remember how they'd send out notices, for the mortars shook the island—we'd open our windows, take any china and glassware off the*

C.A. Boucher, head of the Fort Moultrie Y.M.C.A., in 1906.

shelves in preparedness for the shaking."

Target practice at Fort Moultrie may have shaken the island's china; World War I shook the world. As hostilities broke out in Europe, American leaders took yet another look at defenses along the Atlantic coast. At Fort Moultrie there were only enough troops to man three batteries and protect the mines. Five companies of the South Carolina National Guard were quickly organized to support the Sullivans Island positions. Two months after Germany reopened unrestricted submarine warfare against shipping around the British Isles in February 1917, the United States entered the war. During the next year and a half, a steady stream of recruits trained at Moultrie. By the summer of 1918 an antisubmarine net had been placed across Charleston Harbor to keep out the feared German U-boats, which came as near as North Carolina's Cape Hatteras.

Ever since the Wright brothers' pioneering flight near that cape in 1903, a new type of fighting had rapidly developed: aerial combat. Threats of airplane and zeppelin bombings forced the Coast Artillery to place antiaircraft guns at fortifications up and down the eastern seaboard, including Fort Moultrie. But these were never used in battle, for by late 1918, after savage trench warfare in France and Italy, the "Great War" finally ground to a halt. Germany and its allies had been defeated after great sacrifice and international trauma. The United States demobilized rapidly. By October 1919, 280 men occupied Fort Moultrie facilities which had recently housed 3,000 persons. The two Armstrong rapid-fire guns at Battery Bingham were declared obsolete and given for display in public parks to Paducah, Kentucky, and Burlington, North Carolina.

During the 20 years between the two World Wars, Fort Moultrie was manned by units of the Coast Artillery and the 8th U.S. Infantry, supported by detachments from the Ordnance Service, Financial Department, Quartermaster, and Medical Corps. This garrison soon found itself training a new kind of soldier, the "civilian-soldier" or "civvie." The National Defense Act of 1920 provided for these citizen-soldiers to supplement the 150,000-man Regular Army. In an emergency, the newly trained units could mobilize rapidly. One of these units was the Organized Officers Reserve Corps, which in 1925 began yearly two-week programs at Fort Moultrie. Throughout this intensive encampment approximately 100 officers participated in map sessions, gun drills, calisthenics, and leadership classes.

Most of the civvies were members of the National Guard. Beginning in the summer of 1926, Coast Artillery units from North Carolina (the 252d), South Carolina (the 263d), and Georgia (the 264th) arrived at Fort Moultrie and encamped for about two weeks. These regiments, numbering about 300 men, were sheltered in wall tents, eight guardsmen to a tent. The 252d and 264th drilled on 155-mm guns and practiced subcaliber firing with 37-mm pieces. The 263d, which manned the larger guns and the searchlights, shelled frame targets thousands of yards out to sea. Batteries Jasper and Logan were used frequently, mortar Batteries Capron and Butler only occasionally. Members of the Senior Reserve Officers Training Corps engaged in similar activity. From 1927 into the early 1930s the ROTC attended an annual six-week summer camp at Moultrie and fired the heavy guns.

Citizen's Military Training Camps, begun in the summer of 1927, brought a month of liveliness to the post on Sullivans Island. An average of 600 youths from Georgia and the Carolinas, aged 17 to 29, camped at Fort Moultrie's "tent city" and learned about military life. These young men were divided into four groups—Basic, Red, White, and Blue—based upon experience and previous camps attended. The trainees participated in calisthenics, military exercises, vigorous recreation, and an "acid test" involving an 11-mile hike under the August sun. At the end of camp, the older youths were examined by officers of the 8th infantry and evaluated as possible 2d lieutenants for the Army Reserve. From 1933 until 1939 thousands of other young men were organized on Sullivans Island into companies of the Civilian Conservation Corps. The CCC camps in National Forests and Parks, established by President Franklin D. Roosevelt to help relieve the country from the Depression, owed much to such conditioning centers as the one near Fort Moultrie.

An officer named George C. Marshall had established effective CCC programs in Florida and Georgia. In June 1933 Colonel Marshall arrived at Moultrie to take command of the 8th U.S. Infantry. By this

time Fort Moultrie had grown into a large post, complete with theater, fire station, chapel, service club, stables, and a pavilion. Marshall and his wife moved into a "huge and rather dilapidated" quarters; its 42 French windows required 325 yards of curtain material. Marshall, who brought to his work an exceptional talent for organization, persuaded the Works Progress Administration to aid in rehabilitating the post. In October 1933 Marshall was reassigned to Illinois. At a farewell band concert on Sullivans Island, he told his staff: "I am going places."

The regulars at Fort Moultrie considered the quality of life at the post to be well above average. Morning drills and afternoon school were offset by Thanksgiving turkey shoots, Christmas banquets, and inter-post sports leagues. "On payday nights," notes historian Edwin Bearss, "poker, 21, and craps were a way of life in the barracks." And of course Charleston lay within easy reach after the Cooper River Bridge to Mount Pleasant was opened in 1929.

In September 1939, a genuine menace made itself felt in Europe as Adolf Hitler and his National Socialists—Nazis—overran Poland. A year later, Americans received daily news of the Battle of Britain, fought in the skies against the awesome *Luftwaffe* and in the Atlantic against German U-boats. Meanwhile, the United States began its first peacetime draft, and many National Guard units were called into service. The 252d North Carolina went to Fort Moultrie and camped in tent city. They made preparations to use the big 155-mm guns, which had a barrel nearly 20 feet long and a range of over 10 miles. The 263d South Carolina arrived at Moultrie in early 1941. They mounted searchlights and manned harbor defenses while the Navy positioned an anti-submarine net.

As Hitler's armies rolled on, the need for a coordinated system of harbor defense became clearer. On June 23, 1941, a day after Germany invaded the Soviet Union, the Harbor Entrance Control Posts were authorized. The HECPs were to be jointly manned by the Army and Navy to "operate the elements of the harbor defense." At Charleston both the HECP and the Army's own Harbor Defense Command Post occupied the old two-story signal building on Fort Moultrie's northwest bastion and contained some of the country's most sophisticated military equipment.

George C. Marshall served only five months at Fort Moultrie in 1933 but did much to rehabilitate what had by then become a large and sprawling post. In 1939 he was made Army Chief of Staff and directed the war against the Axis powers. **Left:** *These scenes at Fort Moultrie in the 1940s show, top to bottom, the 252nd Coast Artillery, North Carolina National Guard, firing a 155-mm gun on the beach of Sullivans Island; the "tent city" that housed a constant stream of recruits; and one of the substantial barracks used to house some of the fort's enlisted men.*

These members of the Women's Army Corps were among the last troops to leave Fort Moultrie when the post was deactivated in 1947, ending a tradition of service here that stretched back almost 200 years.

During the American Revolution, women at Fort Moultrie were known as "camp followers." These were usually women of good repute, mostly soldiers' wives, who cooked for the garrison and occasionally made or mended clothing. Normally two camp followers attended each company. Some received extra pay for nursing.

Though efforts to establish quarters on post for women to serve as laundresses were consistently unsuccessful over the years, Fort Moultrie trainees of the 1930s benefited from the nearby Hostess House, which offered opportunities for "recreation and solitude away from the duties of the camp."

The first official recognition of women in military service came shortly after the start of World War II with the creation of the Women's Army Corps. WACs underwent a 6-week basic training program similar to that of their male counterparts. From 1943 onward, WACs served at Fort Moultrie as post vehicle drivers, hospital attendants, and headquarters clerks.

When the Japanese bombed Pearl Harbor on December 7 and plunged America into war, security was tightened throughout the harbor.

On December 11, 1941, Germany declared war on the United States. A month later, U-boats torpedoed several British and American merchant ships near Cape Hatteras. Within weeks the Eastern Sea Frontier amounted to a no-man's land. For the next 10 months, attacks by German U-boats presented a serious threat to shipping along the Atlantic coast. In September 1942, U-455 laid a dozen mines at the entrance to Charleston Harbor, but minesweepers soon detected them and cleared the approaches. During the next months the Allies strengthened their defenses against submarines and, with the effective use of armed convoys and patrol planes, began to turn the tide of battle.

As World War II covered the globe with combat, America's coastal defenses were again modernized. New batteries of heavy artillery were surrounded with a shell of reinforced concrete and earth. Construction No. 520, mounting two 12-inch rifles, was of this sort, along with construction No. 230 between Batteries Logan and Jasper. At Jasper, and at Huger across the harbor in Sumter, 90-mm antiaircraft guns were mounted to defend against small craft as well as strikes from the air. Although a pair of 6-inch guns intended for No. 230 never arrived, the emplacement—shellroom, electric generator, magazine—was encased in concrete. In 1943 and 1944 the Army built a new structure of reinforced concrete at Fort Moultrie to house the HECP-HDCP. By this time, the Allies were winning the war. The Japanese navy had been crippled in the Pacific; the German army was being driven back along all fronts. With victory in sight, demobilization at Moultrie began.

The war meant change for military strategy and tactics. It had proved the practicality of amphibious invasions all along a shore line, not necessarily at harbors or ports. This tactic and the development of carrier aircraft made coastal fortifications obsolete. By 1947 the post at Fort Moultrie was deactivated. Although this and similar forts were no longer needed for the defense of the United States, their history would live on in the imagination and memory of many citizens.

Part 2

Fort Moultrie Today

From Army Reservation to National Park

In 1947, two years after the end of World War II, the Army lowered Fort Moultrie's flag for the last time. Improving military technology had made the concept of static defenses at harbor entrances obsolete. The land and all of the structures formerly owned by the Federal Government on Sullivans Island, except the U.S. Coast Guard station, were sold to private individuals or turned over to the State of South Carolina. Through the years the fort and gun batteries up and down the island gradually deteriorated and became a dangerous playground for children and visitors.

On September 7, 1960, South Carolina transferred the old fort, along with Battery Jasper and an unfinished World War II gun battery known only by its blueprint name, "Construction 230," to the National Park Service. Shortly thereafter, maintenance crews began a massive cleanup and rangers inaugurated visitor tours.

Since the fort on Sullivans Island figured prominently in the Revolutionary War, the National Park Service completed a major restoration in 1976 as a key project of the Bicentennial celebration. In 171 years Fort Moultrie had changed dramatically many times, reflecting advances in military and naval engineering and ordnance. Rather than restore the fort to its appearance at any one particular time in its long history, the Park Service took advantage of a unique opportunity to retain the sites, batteries, and other buildings from many different historic periods which clearly marked the development of seacoast defense from 1776 to 1947. Today you may figuratively walk back in time from the Second World War to the American Revolution and trace many of the changes both in our attitudes toward coast defense and in the fortifications and weapons which implemented our policies.

Fort Moultrie (administered as part of Fort Sumter National Monument) is on West Middle Street on Sullivans Island. To reach it from Charleston, take U.S. 17 N (business) to Mount Pleasant and turn right on SC 703. At Sullivans Island, turn right on Middle Stret. The fort is located 1.5 miles from the intersection.

The following guide highlights the main historical portions of Fort Moultrie today. Begin your tour at the visitor center, then follow the route inside the fort. Refer to the painting on pages 74-75 for orientation. Please watch your step and exercise reasonable caution in the fort. We ask that you use the paths and do not climb the mounds.

Hours of operation can be ascertained by calling (803) 883-3123, or by writing the Superintendent, c/o Fort Sumter National Monument, 1214 Middle Street, Sullivans Island, SC 29482.

Things to Look for at Fort Moultrie

Osceola's Grave and Patapsco Monument Near the entrance to Fort Moultrie are two graves. Enclosed by an iron railing and covered by a marble slab is the grave of the celebrated war leader of the Seminoles Osceola, who died while in confinement at Fort Moultrie on January 30, 1838. Nearby is the monument marking the graves of five of 62 seamen who lost their lives on January 15, 1865, when the U.S. monitor *Patapsco* struck a Confederate torpedo and sank midway between Forts Sumter and Moultrie.

Sally Port Like other exposed masonry of Fort Moultrie, the original entrance way was demolished by Federal artillery fire during the Civil War. This new sally port was completed in 1875. Inside, on the left and right, were enclosed casemates designed to serve as guardrooms for the small detachments normally posted at the fort during peacetime.

HECP/HDCP The camouflaged Harbor Entrance Control Post/Harbor Defense Command Post, completed in March 1944, was jointly operated by the Army and Navy in coordinating the various components of Charleston's harbor defense system. From the upper decks Navy signalmen employed visual signals, including flags and lights, to control access to the harbor. Army personnel, in the nerve center below, stood ready to take immediate defensive action should enemy forces attempt to penetrate the defenses.

The Fort Today

Throughout its long history, Fort Moultrie has undergone numerous changes as improving military and engineering technology added to the complexities of harbor defense. Instead of looking as it did at any one particular period, the fort has been restored to reflect these changes from the camouflaged Harbor Entrance Control Post of World War II to the site of the palmetto log fort of 1776.

The following labels identify the main features of the fort today. Each is keyed by number to the painting below.

74

1/Osceola's Grave and
   Patapsco Monument
2/Sally Port
3/Harbor Entrance Control
   Post/Harbor Defense
   Command Post, 1944-5
4/Harbor Defense
   Batteries, 1898-1939
5/Principal Magazine,
   1870s
6/Service Magazine,
   1870s
7/Post-Civil War Batteries,
   1870-98
8/Civil War Batteries
9/Fort Moultrie III
   Batteries, 1809-60
10/Barracks Foundations,
    1809-63
11/Parade Ground
12/Powder Magazine,
    1809
13/Traverse
14/Postern Gate
15/Approximate site of
    Fort Moultrie II,
    1798-1804
16/Approximate site of
    Fort Moultrie I,
    1776-84

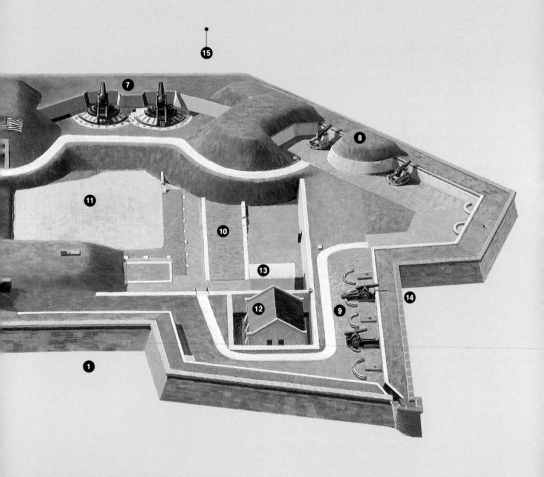

Harbor Defense Batteries, 1898-1939 An integral part of the 1885 Endicott system of harbor defense was the emplacement of light artillery to protect a minefield stretching across Charleston Harbor. These rapid-fire batteries of 4.7-inch and 15-pounder rifles could be pointed, loaded, and fired several times each minute. The outbreak of war with Spain in 1898 spurred Army engineers to complete these positions. Ironically, none of the guns was installed until two months after hostilities ended!

Post-Civil War Batteries, 1870-98 In the 1870s, after rifled artillery had rendered masonry fortifications obsolete, Army engineers undertook to modify Fort Moultrie to meet the threat posed by the new weapon. Huge cannon, including two vintage 15-inch Rodmans capable of cracking the armor plate of naval vessels 4½ miles away, were emplaced within the fort. Adjacent earth-covered concrete ammunition storage rooms were built to withstand the impact of heavy naval artillery.

Civil War Batteries To cope with the dramatic changes in weaponry, particularly rifled cannon, Confederate forces occupying Fort Moultrie between 1861 and 1865 converted it into a massive and extremely powerful earthwork. They covered the walls with sand, mounted guns such as the 10-inch smoothbore and the rifled and banded 8-inch columbiad here today, and built traverses between each cannon to protect the gunners. These measures helped keep Federal forces at bay for nearly two years.

Fort Moultrie III Batteries, 1809-60
This section of the fort represents the appearance of the third Fort Moultrie. Originally mounting 40 guns, its earth-filled masonry walls stood untested during the War of 1812. In 1842 the fort's armament was augmented by larger and more powerful 32-pounder cannon, identical to the ones seen here today. Upon completion of Fort Sumter, directly across the harbor, the two forts could provide a deadly cross-fire that an enemy would hesitate to challenge.

Powder Magazine, 1809 This structure, completed in 1809, is the oldest building in the fort and once housed the fort's entire supply of black powder. In 1861 Moultrie's Confederate garrison covered it with layers of sand and earth as added protection from the heavy Federal artillery. When the principal magazine of the 1870s was constructed near the center of the fort, the Army used this building for storage until 1947. A solid masonry traverse protected the entrance way from the enemy projectiles.

Battery Jasper, constructed in 1898, was (with Batteries Bingham and McCorkle inside Fort Moultrie) part of an attempt to integrate heavy coast artillery, minefields, and rapid-fire weapons into an effective system of coastal defense. Four 10-inch rifles mounted on disappearing carriages recoiled behind the fort's walls after each shot. Regular coast artillery units and National Guardsmen drilled with the rifles until 1943, when they were replaced by 90-mm guns positioned in front of the battery.

Of Related Interest

Fort Sumter stands on a manmade island just over a mile from Fort Moultrie. It was begun in 1829 as part of our Nation's third system of fortifications and designed to play a vital role in Charleston's defense. When completed the five-sided, three-tiered brick structure mounted 135 guns and towered 50 feet above the water. When combined with the guns of Fort Moultrie, a deadly crossfire would effectively seal the harbor entrance, denying access to enemy vessels.

At first construction was slow and difficult, delayed by periods of insufficient funds and a sandbar that required a foundation of thousands of tons of granite before work on the superstructure could begin. Finally, during the mid-1840s, workmen began laying the first of seven million bricks, and by 1860, as the sections of the country appeared to be heading on a collision course, the fort was nearly 90 percent complete.

In November 1860 Maj. Robert Anderson, a Kentuckian and distinguished officer in the Regular Army, was sent to Charleston with the unenviable task of protecting all Federal property in the city, including the harbor forts. Following the secession of South Carolina on December 20, Major Anderson saw the vulnerability of his headquarters at Fort Moultrie and six days later moved his tiny garrison to the still incomplete Sumter. There, he and the 85 officers and men of the 1st United States Artillery began a tense vigil as Southern forces erected batteries completely encircling the harbor fort.

At 4:30 a.m., April 12, 1861, a mortar shell fired from Fort Johnson on James Island illuminated the dawn sky over Sumter, signaling to the other Confederate batteries that the time for action had come. For 34 hours the bombardment of Fort Sumter continued. On April 13, the second day of the battle, Confederate incendiaries and red hot cannon balls set Sumter ablaze and Anderson realized he had no choice but to surrender. The following day victorious Southern troops marched into Sumter. For the next four years Confederate forces defended the fort against Union naval attacks, amphibious assaults, and bombardments by heavy rifled artillery which doomed masony forts like Sumter.

By February 1865 Gen. William T. Sherman's Union army had cut South Carolina in half, effectively trapping the Southern defenders of Charleston Harbor between one Union force to the east and Sherman's to the west. Accordingly, evacuation orders were issued for the night of February 17. Federal troops reoccupied Sumter the following day without firing a shot.

Virtually demolished in the Civil War, Sumter was partially rebuilt and rearmed in the 1870s. In 1898 Battery Huger, a reinforced concrete fortification mounting powerful 12-inch breech-loading guns, was built across Sumter's parade and remained in service until midway through World War II.

Today the fort is a national monument and contains a museum recounting its history to the end of the Civil War. Hours of operation and tour boat schedules are available at the Fort Moultrie visitor center.

☆GPO: 1985—461-442/20002

A Note on Sources

The following unpublished reports by NPS research-historian Edwin C. Bearss provide an informative survey of Fort Moultrie's past: "The Battle of Sullivans Island and the Capture of Fort Moultrie" (1968); "The First Two Fort Moultries: A Structural History" (1968); "Fort Moultrie HECP-HDCP" (1974); and "Fort Moultrie No. 3" (1974). All are solidly based on primary sources.

Important first-hand accounts include William Moultrie, *Memoirs of the American Revolution* (1802); Abner Doubleday, *Reminiscences of Forts Sumter and Moultrie in 1860-'61* (1876); and Erasmus D. Keyes, *Fifty Years' Observation of Men and Events* (1884). Material pertinent to Civil War operations in and around Charleston Harbor is contained in *The War of the Rebellion: A Compilation of the Official Records of the Union and Confederate Armies,* volumes 1, 14, 28, 35, and 47, and in volume 16 of its counterpart series, the *Official Records of the Union and Confederate Navies.*

Emanuel R. Lewis' superb *Seacoast Fortifications of the United States: An Introductory History* (1970) supplies background on a long-neglected subject. Charleston's first century receives deserved attention in three important works by Carl Bridenbaugh: *Cities in the Wilderness: The First Century of Urban Life in America, 1625-1742* (1938); *Cities in Revolt: Urban Life in America, 1743-1776* (1955); and *Myths and Realities: Societies of the Colonial South* (1952). Significant episodes in Moultrie's past are covered in Richard Walsh, *Charleston's Sons of Liberty* (1959) and W. W. Freehling, *Prelude to Civil War: The Nullification Controversy in South Carolina, 1816-1838* (1966).

Illustration Credits

Atlas to Accompany the Official Records of the Union and Confederate Armies: 48 (map); William A. Bake: 70-71, 77 (top), 79; Colonial Williamsburg: cover; *Frank Leslie's Illustrated Newspaper:* 45 (top & bottom); George C. Marshall Research Foundation: 67; Gibbs Art Gallery, Charleston: 6, 8, 9, 24-25; *Harpers Weekly:* 42, 45 (middle); Library of Congress: 20, 38, 40, 41, 43, 49, 55, 59 (Rodman); Museum of Early Southern Decorative Arts, Winston-Salem: 10-11; Museum of the Confederacy, Richmond: 4-5, 52-53 (all); National Archives: 30-31 (all), 58-59, 60 (bottom); National Maritime Museum, London: 15; Naval History Division: 12; New York Public Library: 19; Office of the Chief of Engineers/National Archives: 60 (middle); R. W. Norton Art Gallery, Shreveport: 14; U.S. Army: 62-63; West Point Museum Collection, U.S. Military Academy: 34 (Macomb); Mrs. Lydia Fromberger: 64; Col. Johnson Hagood: 60 (top).